Data Science Team
Complete Self-Assessment Gu

C000133138

The guidance in this Self-Assessment
practices and standards in business process architecture, design and
quality management. The guidance is also based on the professional
judgment of the individual collaborators listed in the Acknowledgments.

Table of Contents

About The Art of Service

The Art of Service, Business Process Architects since 2000, is dedicated to helping stakeholders achieve excellence.

Defining, designing, creating, and implementing a process to solve a stakeholders challenge or meet an objective is the most valuable role… In EVERY group, company, organization and department.

Unless you're talking a one-time, single-use project, there should be a process. Whether that process is managed and implemented by humans, AI, or a combination of the two, it needs to be designed by someone with a complex enough perspective to ask the right questions.

Someone capable of asking the right questions and step back and say, 'What are we really trying to accomplish here? And is there a different way to look at it?'

With The Art of Service's Standard Requirements Self-Assessments, we empower people who can do just that — whether their title is marketer, entrepreneur, manager, salesperson, consultant, Business Process Manager, executive assistant, IT Manager, CIO etc... —they are the people who rule the future. They are people who watch the process as it happens, and ask the right questions to make the process work better.

Contact us when you need any support with this Self-Assessment and any help with templates, blue-prints and examples of standard documents you might need:

http://theartofservice.com
service@theartofservice.com

Included Resources - how to access

Included with your purchase of the book is the Data Science

Team Self-Assessment Spreadsheet Dashboard which contains all questions and Self-Assessment areas and auto-generates insights, graphs, and project RACI planning - all with examples to get you started right away.

How? Simply send an email to
access@theartofservice.com
with this books' title in the subject to get the Data Science Team Self Assessment Tool right away.

You will receive the following contents with New and Updated specific criteria:

- The latest quick edition of the book in PDF

- The latest complete edition of the book in PDF, which criteria correspond to the criteria in...

- The Self-Assessment Excel Dashboard, and...

- Example pre-filled Self-Assessment Excel Dashboard to get familiar with results generation

- In-depth specific Checklists covering the topic

- Project management checklists and templates to assist with implementation

INCLUDES LIFETIME SELF ASSESSMENT UPDATES

Every self assessment comes with Lifetime Updates and Lifetime Free Updated Books. Lifetime Updates is an industry-first feature which allows you to receive verified self assessment updates, ensuring you always have the most accurate information at your fingertips.

Get it now- you will be glad you did - do it now, before you forget.

Send an email to **access@theartofservice.com** with this books' title in the subject to get the Data Science Team Self Assessment Tool right away.

Purpose of this Self-Assessment

This Self-Assessment has been developed to improve understanding of the requirements and elements of Data Science Team, based on best practices and standards in business process architecture, design and quality management.

It is designed to allow for a rapid Self-Assessment to determine how closely existing management practices and procedures correspond to the elements of the Self-Assessment.

The criteria of requirements and elements of Data Science Team have been rephrased in the format of a Self-Assessment questionnaire, with a seven-criterion scoring system, as explained in this document.

In this format, even with limited background knowledge of Data Science Team, a manager can quickly review existing operations to determine how they measure up to the standards. This in turn can serve as the starting point of a 'gap analysis' to identify management tools or system elements that might usefully be implemented in the organization to help improve overall performance.

How to use the Self-Assessment

On the following pages are a series of questions to identify to what extent your Data Science Team initiative is complete in comparison to the requirements set in standards.

To facilitate answering the questions, there is a space in front of each question to enter a score on a scale of '1' to '5'.

1 Strongly Disagree

2 Disagree

3 Neutral

4 Agree

5 Strongly Agree

Read the question and rate it with the following in front of mind:

'In my belief,
the answer to this question is clearly defined'.

There are two ways in which you can choose to interpret this statement;
1. how aware are you that the answer to the question is clearly defined
2. for more in-depth analysis you can choose to gather evidence and confirm the answer to the question. This obviously will take more time, most Self-Assessment users opt for the first way to interpret the question and dig deeper later on based on the outcome of the overall Self-Assessment.

A score of '1' would mean that the answer is not clear at all, where a '5' would mean the answer is crystal clear and defined. Leave emtpy when the question is not applicable or you don't want to answer it, you can skip it without affecting your score. Write your score in the space provided.

After you have responded to all the appropriate statements in each section, compute your average score for that section, using the formula provided, and round to the nearest tenth. Then transfer to the corresponding spoke in the Data Science Team Scorecard on the second next page of the Self-Assessment.

Your completed Data Science Team Scorecard will give you a clear presentation of which Data Science Team areas need attention.

Data Science Team
Scorecard Example

Example of how the finalized Scorecard can look like:

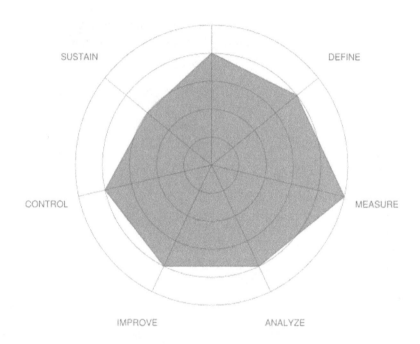

Data Science Team Scorecard

Your Scores:

BEGINNING OF THE SELF-ASSESSMENT:

CRITERION #1: RECOGNIZE

INTENT: Be aware of the need for change. Recognize that there is an unfavorable variation, problem or symptom.

In my belief, the answer to this question is clearly defined:

5 Strongly Agree

4 Agree

3 Neutral

2 Disagree

1 Strongly Disagree

1. Is it clear when you think of the day ahead of you what activities and tasks you need to complete?
<--- Score

2. Are there regulatory / compliance issues?
<--- Score

3. How are the data science team's objectives aligned to the group's overall stakeholder strategy?

<--- Score

4. Who should resolve the data science team issues?
<--- Score

5. What is the recognized need?
<--- Score

6. How do you assess your data science team workforce capability and capacity needs, including skills, competencies, and staffing levels?
<--- Score

7. Looking at each person individually – does every one have the qualities which are needed to work in this group?
<--- Score

8. Do you recognize data science team achievements?
<--- Score

9. Will new equipment/products be required to facilitate data science team delivery, for example is new software needed?
<--- Score

10. Who needs budgets?
<--- Score

11. Is the quality assurance team identified?
<--- Score

12. What do you need to start doing?
<--- Score

13. Who needs what information?

<--- Score

14. Where do you need to exercise leadership?
<--- Score

15. Are employees recognized for desired behaviors?
<--- Score

16. What prevents you from making the changes you know will make you a more effective data science team leader?
<--- Score

17. What needs to stay?
<--- Score

18. How are you going to measure success?
<--- Score

19. What data science team events should you attend?
<--- Score

20. Which needs are not included or involved?
<--- Score

21. Does data science team create potential expectations in other areas that need to be recognized and considered?
<--- Score

22. Are losses recognized in a timely manner?
<--- Score

23. As a sponsor, customer or management, how important is it to meet goals, objectives?
<--- Score

24. What does data science team success mean to the stakeholders?
<--- Score

25. What extra resources will you need?
<--- Score

26. What are the timeframes required to resolve each of the issues/problems?
<--- Score

27. How do you recognize an data science team objection?
<--- Score

28. Are there any specific expectations or concerns about the data science team team, data science team itself?
<--- Score

29. How much are sponsors, customers, partners, stakeholders involved in data science team? In other words, what are the risks, if data science team does not deliver successfully?
<--- Score

30. What situation(s) led to this data science team Self Assessment?
<--- Score

31. Do you need to avoid or amend any data science team activities?
<--- Score

32. To what extent does each concerned units

management team recognize data science team as an effective investment?
<--- Score

33. Do you have/need 24-hour access to key personnel?
<--- Score

34. Think about the people you identified for your data science team project and the project responsibilities you would assign to them, what kind of training do you think they would need to perform these responsibilities effectively?
<--- Score

35. How do you take a forward-looking perspective in identifying data science team research related to market response and models?
<--- Score

36. Will a response program recognize when a crisis occurs and provide some level of response?
<--- Score

37. Where is training needed?
<--- Score

38. What training and capacity building actions are needed to implement proposed reforms?
<--- Score

39. Does your organization need more data science team education?
<--- Score

40. How do you recognize an objection?

<--- Score

41. What information do users need?
<--- Score

42. What are the minority interests and what amount of minority interests can be recognized?
<--- Score

43. Do you know what you need to know about data science team?
<--- Score

44. How do you identify the kinds of information that you will need?
<--- Score

45. What should be considered when identifying available resources, constraints, and deadlines?
<--- Score

46. What is the smallest subset of the problem you can usefully solve?
<--- Score

47. Why the need?
<--- Score

48. Consider your own data science team project, what types of organizational problems do you think might be causing or affecting your problem, based on the work done so far?
<--- Score

49. How does it fit into your organizational needs and tasks?

<--- Score

50. Do you need different information or graphics?
<--- Score

51. What is the data science team problem definition? What do you need to resolve?
<--- Score

52. What are the clients issues and concerns?
<--- Score

53. Are there any revenue recognition issues?
<--- Score

54. What are your needs in relation to data science team skills, labor, equipment, and markets?
<--- Score

55. Are problem definition and motivation clearly presented?
<--- Score

56. Why is this needed?
<--- Score

57. What do employees need in the short term?
<--- Score

58. How many trainings, in total, are needed?
<--- Score

59. Are your goals realistic? Do you need to redefine your problem? Perhaps the problem has changed or maybe you have reached your goal and need to set a new one?

<--- Score

60. What else needs to be measured?
<--- Score

61. Will it solve real problems?
<--- Score

62. Which information does the data science team business case need to include?
<--- Score

63. For your data science team project, identify and describe the business environment, is there more than one layer to the business environment?
<--- Score

64. What resources or support might you need?
<--- Score

65. What is the problem or issue?
<--- Score

66. When a data science team manager recognizes a problem, what options are available?
<--- Score

67. Are you dealing with any of the same issues today as yesterday? What can you do about this?
<--- Score

68. How can auditing be a preventative security measure?
<--- Score

69. What are the expected benefits of data science

team to the stakeholder?
<--- Score

70. Are there recognized data science team problems?
<--- Score

71. Who defines the rules in relation to any given issue?
<--- Score

72. Will data science team deliverables need to be tested and, if so, by whom?
<--- Score

73. Have you identified your data science team key performance indicators?
<--- Score

74. What is the extent or complexity of the data science team problem?
<--- Score

75. Would you recognize a threat from the inside?
<--- Score

76. What problems are you facing and how do you consider data science team will circumvent those obstacles?
<--- Score

77. Who needs to know about data science team?
<--- Score

78. What is the problem and/or vulnerability?
<--- Score

79. What are the data science team resources needed?
<--- Score

80. Can management personnel recognize the monetary benefit of data science team?
<--- Score

81. Are controls defined to recognize and contain problems?
<--- Score

82. What tools and technologies are needed for a custom data science team project?
<--- Score

83. What would happen if data science team weren't done?
<--- Score

84. Does the problem have ethical dimensions?
<--- Score

85. Are employees recognized or rewarded for performance that demonstrates the highest levels of integrity?
<--- Score

86. Did you miss any major data science team issues?
<--- Score

87. Whom do you really need or want to serve?
<--- Score

88. What activities does the governance board need to consider?
<--- Score

89. Who else hopes to benefit from it?
<--- Score

90. What are the stakeholder objectives to be achieved with data science team?
<--- Score

91. How do you identify subcontractor relationships?
<--- Score

92. Which issues are too important to ignore?
<--- Score

93. How are training requirements identified?
<--- Score

94. Are there data science team problems defined?
<--- Score

95. Who needs to know?
<--- Score

96. Is the need for organizational change recognized?
<--- Score

97. Is it needed?
<--- Score

98. What data science team coordination do you need?
<--- Score

99. To what extent would your organization benefit from being recognized as a award recipient?
<--- Score

100. Who are your key stakeholders who need to sign off?
<--- Score

101. What needs to be done?
<--- Score

102. What data science team problem should be solved?
<--- Score

103. What creative shifts do you need to take?
<--- Score

Add up total points for this section:
_ _ _ _ _ = Total points for this section

Divided by: _ _ _ _ _ _ (number of statements answered) = _ _ _ _ _ _
Average score for this section

Transfer your score to the data science team Index at the beginning of the Self-Assessment.

CRITERION #2: DEFINE:

INTENT: Formulate the stakeholder problem. Define the problem, needs and objectives.

In my belief, the answer to this question is clearly defined:

5 Strongly Agree

4 Agree

3 Neutral

2 Disagree

1 Strongly Disagree

1. What is in scope?
<--- Score

2. Who is gathering data science team information?
<--- Score

3. If substitutes have been appointed, have they been briefed on the data science team goals and received regular communications as to the progress to date?

<--- Score

4. Are the data science team requirements complete?
<--- Score

5. Are the data science team requirements testable?
<--- Score

6. What are the tasks and definitions?
<--- Score

7. Has a high-level 'as is' process map been completed, verified and validated?
<--- Score

8. What specifically is the problem? Where does it occur? When does it occur? What is its extent?
<--- Score

9. How do you gather the stories?
<--- Score

10. What scope to assess?
<--- Score

11. How will the data science team team and the group measure complete success of data science team?
<--- Score

12. Is the team adequately staffed with the desired cross-functionality? If not, what additional resources are available to the team?
<--- Score

13. When is the estimated completion date?

<--- Score

14. What are the Roles and Responsibilities for each team member and its leadership? Where is this documented?
<--- Score

15. What is the definition of success?
<--- Score

16. Has the direction changed at all during the course of data science team? If so, when did it change and why?
<--- Score

17. Are different versions of process maps needed to account for the different types of inputs?
<--- Score

18. Is there a completed SIPOC representation, describing the Suppliers, Inputs, Process, Outputs, and Customers?
<--- Score

19. How do you build the right business case?
<--- Score

20. How will variation in the actual durations of each activity be dealt with to ensure that the expected data science team results are met?
<--- Score

21. What is the worst case scenario?
<--- Score

22. Are accountability and ownership for data science

team clearly defined?
<--- Score

23. Do you have a data science team success story or case study ready to tell and share?
<--- Score

24. Who approved the data science team scope?
<--- Score

25. What is out of scope?
<--- Score

26. What are the dynamics of the communication plan?
<--- Score

27. How do you hand over data science team context?
<--- Score

28. Has anyone else (internal or external to the group) attempted to solve this problem or a similar one before? If so, what knowledge can be leveraged from these previous efforts?
<--- Score

29. Are roles and responsibilities formally defined?
<--- Score

30. Is the current 'as is' process being followed? If not, what are the discrepancies?
<--- Score

31. What is the scope of data science team?
<--- Score

32. Have specific policy objectives been defined?
<--- Score

33. Scope of sensitive information?
<--- Score

34. Who is gathering information?
<--- Score

35. Do you all define data science team in the same way?
<--- Score

36. Does the scope remain the same?
<--- Score

37. Are task requirements clearly defined?
<--- Score

38. Has your scope been defined?
<--- Score

39. What is a worst-case scenario for losses?
<--- Score

40. Has/have the customer(s) been identified?
<--- Score

41. What sort of initial information to gather?
<--- Score

42. What data science team services do you require?
<--- Score

43. What sources do you use to gather information for a data science team study?

<--- Score

44. Why are you doing data science team and what is the scope?
<--- Score

45. Do you have organizational privacy requirements?
<--- Score

46. Are there any constraints known that bear on the ability to perform data science team work? How is the team addressing them?
<--- Score

47. What knowledge or experience is required?
<--- Score

48. Is the scope of data science team defined?
<--- Score

49. What would be the goal or target for a data science team's improvement team?
<--- Score

50. What are the core elements of the data science team business case?
<--- Score

51. Have all of the relationships been defined properly?
<--- Score

52. Is special data science team user knowledge required?
<--- Score

53. What is the context?
<--- Score

54. Is scope creep really all bad news?
<--- Score

55. What happens if data science team's scope changes?
<--- Score

56. What defines best in class?
<--- Score

57. Will a data science team production readiness review be required?
<--- Score

58. Is there a critical path to deliver data science team results?
<--- Score

59. Is the data science team scope complete and appropriately sized?
<--- Score

60. What key stakeholder process output measure(s) does data science team leverage and how?
<--- Score

61. Have all basic functions of data science team been defined?
<--- Score

62. What gets examined?
<--- Score

63. What are the boundaries of the scope? What is in bounds and what is not? What is the start point? What is the stop point?
<--- Score

64. What is the scope of the data science team work?
<--- Score

65. What customer feedback methods were used to solicit their input?
<--- Score

66. What are the compelling stakeholder reasons for embarking on data science team?
<--- Score

67. How is the team tracking and documenting its work?
<--- Score

68. In what way can you redefine the criteria of choice clients have in your category in your favor?
<--- Score

69. Who are the data science team improvement team members, including Management Leads and Coaches?
<--- Score

70. Is the work to date meeting requirements?
<--- Score

71. What are the rough order estimates on cost savings/opportunities that data science team brings?
<--- Score

72. How do you manage unclear data science team requirements?
<--- Score

73. Is data science team currently on schedule according to the plan?
<--- Score

74. How do you gather data science team requirements?
<--- Score

75. Does the team have regular meetings?
<--- Score

76. Is the improvement team aware of the different versions of a process: what they think it is vs. what it actually is vs. what it should be vs. what it could be?
<--- Score

77. Is it clearly defined in and to your organization what you do?
<--- Score

78. How do you think the partners involved in data science team would have defined success?
<--- Score

79. Is there regularly 100% attendance at the team meetings? If not, have appointed substitutes attended to preserve cross-functionality and full representation?
<--- Score

80. Is data science team linked to key stakeholder goals and objectives?

<--- Score

81. What constraints exist that might impact the team?
<--- Score

82. What are (control) requirements for data science team Information?
<--- Score

83. What are the data science team use cases?
<--- Score

84. What is the definition of data science team excellence?
<--- Score

85. How have you defined all data science team requirements first?
<--- Score

86. What was the context?
<--- Score

87. How do you keep key subject matter experts in the loop?
<--- Score

88. How are consistent data science team definitions important?
<--- Score

89. What critical content must be communicated – who, what, when, where, and how?
<--- Score

90. Who defines (or who defined) the rules and roles?
<--- Score

91. How do you catch data science team definition inconsistencies?
<--- Score

92. Is the data science team scope manageable?
<--- Score

93. Is there any additional data science team definition of success?
<--- Score

94. How does the data science team manager ensure against scope creep?
<--- Score

95. What are the record-keeping requirements of data science team activities?
<--- Score

96. What scope do you want your strategy to cover?
<--- Score

97. What data science team requirements should be gathered?
<--- Score

98. Is there a clear data science team case definition?
<--- Score

99. Is data science team required?
<--- Score

100. How and when will the baselines be defined?

<--- Score

101. When is/was the data science team start date?
<--- Score

102. Have the customer needs been translated into specific, measurable requirements? How?
<--- Score

103. How often are the team meetings?
<--- Score

104. What intelligence can you gather?
<--- Score

105. Are resources adequate for the scope?
<--- Score

106. Has a team charter been developed and communicated?
<--- Score

107. What are the data science team tasks and definitions?
<--- Score

108. How would you define the culture at your organization, how susceptible is it to data science team changes?
<--- Score

109. Are all requirements met?
<--- Score

110. How did the data science team manager receive input to the development of a data science team

improvement plan and the estimated completion dates/times of each activity?
<--- Score

111. The political context: who holds power?
<--- Score

112. What system do you use for gathering data science team information?
<--- Score

113. What is the scope of the data science team effort?
<--- Score

114. What baselines are required to be defined and managed?
<--- Score

115. How do you manage scope?
<--- Score

116. Has the improvement team collected the 'voice of the customer' (obtained feedback – qualitative and quantitative)?
<--- Score

117. What is out-of-scope initially?
<--- Score

118. Are there different segments of customers?
<--- Score

119. Has the data science team work been fairly and/ or equitably divided and delegated among team members who are qualified and capable to perform the work? Has everyone contributed?

<--- Score

120. Has a data science team requirement not been met?
<--- Score

121. When are meeting minutes sent out? Who is on the distribution list?
<--- Score

122. Has everyone on the team, including the team leaders, been properly trained?
<--- Score

123. Where can you gather more information?
<--- Score

124. What are the requirements for audit information?
<--- Score

125. Do the problem and goal statements meet the SMART criteria (specific, measurable, attainable, relevant, and time-bound)?
<--- Score

126. What information should you gather?
<--- Score

127. What information do you gather?
<--- Score

128. How was the 'as is' process map developed, reviewed, verified and validated?
<--- Score

129. What is in the scope and what is not in scope?

<--- Score

130. Are approval levels defined for contracts and supplements to contracts?
<--- Score

131. How do you manage changes in data science team requirements?
<--- Score

132. Has a project plan, Gantt chart, or similar been developed/completed?
<--- Score

Add up total points for this section:
_____ = Total points for this section

Divided by: _____ (number of statements answered) = _____
Average score for this section

Transfer your score to the data science team Index at the beginning of the Self-Assessment.

CRITERION #3: MEASURE:

INTENT: Gather the correct data.
Measure the current performance and
evolution of the situation.

In my belief, the answer to this
question is clearly defined:

5 Strongly Agree

4 Agree

3 Neutral

2 Disagree

1 Strongly Disagree

1. At what cost?
<--- Score

2. What are your key data science team organizational performance measures, including key short and longer-term financial measures?
<--- Score

3. Are data science team vulnerabilities categorized

and prioritized?
<--- Score

4. What measurements are being captured?
<--- Score

5. What are the types and number of measures to use?
<--- Score

6. What methods are feasible and acceptable to estimate the impact of reforms?
<--- Score

7. Are the units of measure consistent?
<--- Score

8. Are you able to realize any cost savings?
<--- Score

9. What is your data science team quality cost segregation study?
<--- Score

10. What are your operating costs?
<--- Score

11. What is measured? Why?
<--- Score

12. What tests verify requirements?
<--- Score

13. Are actual costs in line with budgeted costs?
<--- Score

14. Have you made assumptions about the shape of

the future, particularly its impact on your customers and competitors?
<--- Score

15. What does a Test Case verify?
<--- Score

16. How is performance measured?
<--- Score

17. How will the data science team data be analyzed?
<--- Score

18. Are you taking your company in the direction of better and revenue or cheaper and cost?
<--- Score

19. How do you measure success?
<--- Score

20. What is your decision requirements diagram?
<--- Score

21. Have design-to-cost goals been established?
<--- Score

22. How sensitive must the data science team strategy be to cost?
<--- Score

23. How can a data science team test verify your ideas or assumptions?
<--- Score

24. How can you manage cost down?
<--- Score

25. How can you reduce the costs of obtaining inputs?
<--- Score

26. Which measures and indicators matter?
<--- Score

27. How do you verify the data science team requirements quality?
<--- Score

28. How is progress measured?
<--- Score

29. What are your customers expectations and measures?
<--- Score

30. How do you verify the authenticity of the data and information used?
<--- Score

31. What do you measure and why?
<--- Score

32. What is the total fixed cost?
<--- Score

33. Will data science team have an impact on current business continuity, disaster recovery processes and/ or infrastructure?
<--- Score

34. How do you aggregate measures across priorities?
<--- Score

35. What users will be impacted?
<--- Score

36. Are you aware of what could cause a problem?
<--- Score

37. Is the cost worth the data science team effort ?
<--- Score

38. What causes mismanagement?
<--- Score

39. What does your operating model cost?
<--- Score

40. What are the data science team key cost drivers?
<--- Score

41. How do you measure efficient delivery of data science team services?
<--- Score

42. Are there competing data science team priorities?
<--- Score

43. How frequently do you verify your data science team strategy?
<--- Score

44. How do you measure variability?
<--- Score

45. Where is it measured?
<--- Score

46. How do you quantify and qualify impacts?

<--- Score

47. What measurements are possible, practicable and meaningful?
<--- Score

48. How will you measure success?
<--- Score

49. What are the strategic priorities for this year?
<--- Score

50. What is the cost of rework?
<--- Score

51. Why do you expend time and effort to implement measurement, for whom?
<--- Score

52. What are the costs and benefits?
<--- Score

53. What are predictive data science team analytics?
<--- Score

54. Does the data science team task fit the client's priorities?
<--- Score

55. How will costs be allocated?
<--- Score

56. What does verifying compliance entail?
<--- Score

57. What happens if cost savings do not materialize?

<--- Score

58. How are measurements made?
<--- Score

59. What are hidden data science team quality costs?
<--- Score

60. Does a data science team quantification method exist?
<--- Score

61. What are the estimated costs of proposed changes?
<--- Score

62. Where can you go to verify the info?
<--- Score

63. What drives O&M cost?
<--- Score

64. What is the cause of any data science team gaps?
<--- Score

65. Was a business case (cost/benefit) developed?
<--- Score

66. How do you verify performance?
<--- Score

67. Is there an opportunity to verify requirements?
<--- Score

68. How do you verify your resources?
<--- Score

69. What is the root cause(s) of the problem?
<--- Score

70. Are missed data science team opportunities costing your organization money?
<--- Score

71. How are you verifying it?
<--- Score

72. Does management have the right priorities among projects?
<--- Score

73. How do you control the overall costs of your work processes?
<--- Score

74. How do you verify data science team completeness and accuracy?
<--- Score

75. Which costs should be taken into account?
<--- Score

76. Are there measurements based on task performance?
<--- Score

77. How will measures be used to manage and adapt?
<--- Score

78. What is the data science team business impact?
<--- Score

79. How is the value delivered by data science team being measured?
<--- Score

80. How can you measure data science team in a systematic way?
<--- Score

81. How can you reduce costs?
<--- Score

82. What could cause delays in the schedule?
<--- Score

83. How can you measure the performance?
<--- Score

84. Among the data science team product and service cost to be estimated, which is considered hardest to estimate?
<--- Score

85. Are the measurements objective?
<--- Score

86. What are the uncertainties surrounding estimates of impact?
<--- Score

87. Are the data science team benefits worth its costs?
<--- Score

88. What are the costs of reform?
<--- Score

89. How do you measure lifecycle phases?

<--- Score

90. What is your cost benefit analysis?
<--- Score

91. How do you verify if data science team is built right?
<--- Score

92. What are allowable costs?
<--- Score

93. What potential environmental factors impact the data science team effort?
<--- Score

94. What relevant entities could be measured?
<--- Score

95. What are you verifying?
<--- Score

96. What would it cost to replace your technology?
<--- Score

97. How to cause the change?
<--- Score

98. What details are required of the data science team cost structure?
<--- Score

99. Has a cost center been established?
<--- Score

100. What is the total cost related to deploying data

science team, including any consulting or professional services?
<--- Score

101. What do people want to verify?
<--- Score

102. How do you focus on what is right -not who is right?
<--- Score

103. Is it possible to estimate the impact of unanticipated complexity such as wrong or failed assumptions, feedback, etcetera on proposed reforms?
<--- Score

104. Did you tackle the cause or the symptom?
<--- Score

105. The approach of traditional data science team works for detail complexity but is focused on a systematic approach rather than an understanding of the nature of systems themselves, what approach will permit your organization to deal with the kind of unpredictable emergent behaviors that dynamic complexity can introduce?
<--- Score

106. How will your organization measure success?
<--- Score

107. Who should receive measurement reports?
<--- Score

108. What are the operational costs after data science

team deployment?
<--- Score

109. When should you bother with diagrams?
<--- Score

110. What are your primary costs, revenues, assets?
<--- Score

111. Do you verify that corrective actions were taken?
<--- Score

112. Why a data science team focus?
<--- Score

113. How much does it cost?
<--- Score

114. How long to keep data and how to manage
retention costs?
<--- Score

115. Where is the cost?
<--- Score

116. How do you verify and validate the data science
team data?
<--- Score

117. What are the costs?
<--- Score

118. When a disaster occurs, who gets priority?
<--- Score

119. Why do the measurements/indicators matter?

<--- Score

120. What is an unallowable cost?
<--- Score

121. Is the scope of data science team cost analysis cost-effective?
<--- Score

122. What would be a real cause for concern?
<--- Score

123. How will you measure your data science team effectiveness?
<--- Score

124. What are the costs of delaying data science team action?
<--- Score

125. How do you stay flexible and focused to recognize larger data science team results?
<--- Score

126. How do you verify and develop ideas and innovations?
<--- Score

127. What could cause you to change course?
<--- Score

128. What can be used to verify compliance?
<--- Score

129. What does losing customers cost your organization?

<--- Score

130. What are the data science team investment costs?
<--- Score

131. Are there any easy-to-implement alternatives to data science team? Sometimes other solutions are available that do not require the cost implications of a full-blown project?
<--- Score

132. What harm might be caused?
<--- Score

133. Is the solution cost-effective?
<--- Score

134. Was a life-cycle cost analysis performed?
<--- Score

135. When are costs are incurred?
<--- Score

136. How do your measurements capture actionable data science team information for use in exceeding your customers expectations and securing your customers engagement?
<--- Score

137. What are the current costs of the data science team process?
<--- Score

138. Who pays the cost?
<--- Score

139. Do the benefits outweigh the costs?
<--- Score

Add up total points for this section:
_____ = Total points for this section

Divided by: _____ (number of
statements answered) = _____
Average score for this section

Transfer your score to the data science
team Index at the beginning of the
Self-Assessment.

CRITERION #4: ANALYZE:

INTENT: Analyze causes, assumptions and hypotheses.

In my belief, the answer to this question is clearly defined:

5 Strongly Agree

4 Agree

3 Neutral

2 Disagree

1 Strongly Disagree

1. What are the processes for audit reporting and management?
<--- Score

2. Identify an operational issue in your organization, for example, could a particular task be done more quickly or more efficiently by data science team?
<--- Score

3. How do you build, nurture and place data

science teams inside your organization?
<--- Score

4. Who owns what data?
<--- Score

5. Has data output been validated?
<--- Score

6. What did the team gain from developing a sub-process map?
<--- Score

7. What quality tools were used to get through the analyze phase?
<--- Score

8. How is the way you as the leader think and process information affecting your organizational culture?
<--- Score

9. What output to create?
<--- Score

10. Do quality systems drive continuous improvement?
<--- Score

11. How do mission and objectives affect the data science team processes of your organization?
<--- Score

12. Where is the data coming from to measure compliance?
<--- Score

13. What is your organizations process which leads to recognition of value generation?
<--- Score

14. What are your data science team processes?
<--- Score

15. Should you invest in industry-recognized qualifications?
<--- Score

16. What successful thing are you doing today that may be blinding you to new growth opportunities?
<--- Score

17. How do you measure the operational performance of your key work systems and processes, including productivity, cycle time, and other appropriate measures of process effectiveness, efficiency, and innovation?
<--- Score

18. Were any designed experiments used to generate additional insight into the data analysis?
<--- Score

19. What is the output?
<--- Score

20. Who will facilitate the team and process?
<--- Score

21. What are the disruptive data science team technologies that enable your organization to radically change your business processes?
<--- Score

22. What are your current levels and trends in key measures or indicators of data science team product and process performance that are important to and directly serve your customers? How do these results compare with the performance of your competitors and other organizations with similar offerings?
<--- Score

23. What are evaluation criteria for the output?
<--- Score

24. How do you promote understanding that opportunity for improvement is not criticism of the status quo, or the people who created the status quo?
<--- Score

25. What data science team data should be managed?
<--- Score

26. What are the revised rough estimates of the financial savings/opportunity for data science team improvements?
<--- Score

27. What qualifications are necessary?
<--- Score

28. What conclusions were drawn from the team's data collection and analysis? How did the team reach these conclusions?
<--- Score

29. What tools were used to generate the list of possible causes?
<--- Score

30. What information qualified as important?
<--- Score

31. What data science team data should be collected?
<--- Score

32. What is the oversight process?
<--- Score

33. What are the necessary qualifications?
<--- Score

34. What other organizational variables, such as reward systems or communication systems, affect the performance of this data science team process?
<--- Score

35. Are data science team changes recognized early enough to be approved through the regular process?
<--- Score

36. What qualifications and skills do you need?
<--- Score

37. How will the change process be managed?
<--- Score

38. Is the gap/opportunity displayed and communicated in financial terms?
<--- Score

39. How do your work systems and key work processes relate to and capitalize on your core competencies?
<--- Score

40. What types of data do your data science team indicators require?
<--- Score

41. Where is data science team data gathered?
<--- Score

42. What are your outputs?
<--- Score

43. What data science team metrics are outputs of the process?
<--- Score

44. Are you missing data science team opportunities?
<--- Score

45. How do you identify specific data science team investment opportunities and emerging trends?
<--- Score

46. What does the data say about the performance of the stakeholder process?
<--- Score

47. How do you use data science team data and information to support organizational decision making and innovation?
<--- Score

48. How often will data be collected for measures?
<--- Score

49. How is the data gathered?
<--- Score

50. What were the financial benefits resulting from any 'ground fruit or low-hanging fruit' (quick fixes)?
<--- Score

51. Was a cause-and-effect diagram used to explore the different types of causes (or sources of variation)?
<--- Score

52. Are your outputs consistent?
<--- Score

53. What methods do you use to gather data science team data?
<--- Score

54. What data science team data do you gather or use now?
<--- Score

55. What is your organizations system for selecting qualified vendors?
<--- Score

56. What are the best opportunities for value improvement?
<--- Score

57. What are your key performance measures or indicators and in-process measures for the control and improvement of your data science team processes?
<--- Score

58. Is data and process analysis, root cause analysis and quantifying the gap/opportunity in place?

<--- Score

59. What are your best practices for minimizing data science team project risk, while demonstrating incremental value and quick wins throughout the data science team project lifecycle?
<--- Score

60. What is the complexity of the output produced?
<--- Score

61. What qualifications are needed?
<--- Score

62. What qualifies as competition?
<--- Score

63. Is the required data science team data gathered?
<--- Score

64. Is the data science team process severely broken such that a re-design is necessary?
<--- Score

65. What tools were used to narrow the list of possible causes?
<--- Score

66. Where can you get qualified talent today?
<--- Score

67. Do your data science teams have best-in-class and highly repeatable processes that produce reliable outputs to the business?
<--- Score

68. What, related to, data science team processes does your organization outsource?
<--- Score

69. What resources go in to get the desired output?
<--- Score

70. When should a process be art not science?
<--- Score

71. Were there any improvement opportunities identified from the process analysis?
<--- Score

72. Are data science teams able to deploy work in various formats (ex: visualizations, reports, model APIs) to meet business needs?
<--- Score

73. What are the personnel training and qualifications required?
<--- Score

74. Are your data science teams using agile approaches (ex: DataOps) for building and deploying data products?
<--- Score

75. What data science team data will be collected?
<--- Score

76. Think about the functions involved in your data science team project, what processes flow from these functions?
<--- Score

77. Who is involved with workflow mapping?
<--- Score

78. What training and qualifications will you need?
<--- Score

79. A compounding model resolution with available relevant data can often provide insight towards a solution methodology; which data science team models, tools and techniques are necessary?
<--- Score

80. How will the data science team data be captured?
<--- Score

81. How can risk management be tied procedurally to process elements?
<--- Score

82. Is the suppliers process defined and controlled?
<--- Score

83. How was the detailed process map generated, verified, and validated?
<--- Score

84. What are the data science team design outputs?
<--- Score

85. Did any value-added analysis or 'lean thinking' take place to identify some of the gaps shown on the 'as is' process map?
<--- Score

86. Have the problem and goal statements been updated to reflect the additional knowledge gained

from the analyze phase?
<--- Score

87. What qualifications do data science team leaders need?
<--- Score

88. Do your employees have the opportunity to do what they do best everyday?
<--- Score

89. What process should you select for improvement?
<--- Score

90. What is the cost of poor quality as supported by the team's analysis?
<--- Score

91. How has the data science team data been gathered?
<--- Score

92. Are gaps between current performance and the goal performance identified?
<--- Score

93. Is the performance gap determined?
<--- Score

94. Have any additional benefits been identified that will result from closing all or most of the gaps?
<--- Score

95. How will the data be checked for quality?
<--- Score

96. Are all staff in core data science team subjects Highly Qualified?
<--- Score

97. What will drive data science team change?
<--- Score

98. Did any additional data need to be collected?
<--- Score

99. Is the final output clearly identified?
<--- Score

100. Is there an established change management process?
<--- Score

101. What are the data science team business drivers?
<--- Score

102. How do you define collaboration and team output?
<--- Score

103. Record-keeping requirements flow from the records needed as inputs, outputs, controls and for transformation of a data science team process, are the records needed as inputs to the data science team process available?
<--- Score

104. How does the organization define, manage, and improve its data science team processes?
<--- Score

105. An organizationally feasible system request is

one that considers the mission, goals and objectives of the organization, key questions are: is the data science team solution request practical and will it solve a problem or take advantage of an opportunity to achieve company goals?
<--- Score

106. Is there a strict change management process?
<--- Score

107. Do your leaders quickly bounce back from setbacks?
<--- Score

108. What systems/processes must you excel at?
<--- Score

109. How much data can be collected in the given timeframe?
<--- Score

110. Which data science team data should be retained?
<--- Score

111. Do several people in different organizational units assist with the data science team process?
<--- Score

112. How do you ensure that the data science team opportunity is realistic?
<--- Score

113. Is there any way to speed up the process?
<--- Score

114. What are your current levels and trends in key data science team measures or indicators of product and process performance that are important to and directly serve your customers?
<--- Score

115. Has an output goal been set?
<--- Score

116. Do staff qualifications match your project?
<--- Score

117. What data is gathered?
<--- Score

118. Who gets your output?
<--- Score

119. Who is involved in the management review process?
<--- Score

120. How difficult is it to qualify what data science team ROI is?
<--- Score

121. Was a detailed process map created to amplify critical steps of the 'as is' stakeholder process?
<--- Score

122. Who will gather what data?
<--- Score

123. Do your contracts/agreements contain data security obligations?
<--- Score

124. What process improvements will be needed?
<--- Score

125. How is the data science team Value Stream Mapping managed?
<--- Score

126. Do you have the authority to produce the output?
<--- Score

127. How many input/output points does it require?
<--- Score

128. How are outputs preserved and protected?
<--- Score

129. How will corresponding data be collected?
<--- Score

130. Were Pareto charts (or similar) used to portray the 'heavy hitters' (or key sources of variation)?
<--- Score

131. How is data science team data gathered?
<--- Score

132. Do you understand your management processes today?
<--- Score

133. What data do you need to collect?
<--- Score

134. Can you add value to the current data science

team decision-making process (largely qualitative) by incorporating uncertainty modeling (more quantitative)?
<--- Score

135. What were the crucial 'moments of truth' on the process map?
<--- Score

136. Who qualifies to gain access to data?
<--- Score

137. How do you implement and manage your work processes to ensure that they meet design requirements?
<--- Score

138. Are all team members qualified for all tasks?
<--- Score

139. Think about some of the processes you undertake within your organization, which do you own?
<--- Score

140. How is data used for program management and improvement?
<--- Score

141. What internal processes need improvement?
<--- Score

Add up total points for this section:
_____ = Total points for this section

Divided by: _____ (number of

statements answered) = _____
Average score for this section

Transfer your score to the data science
team Index at the beginning of the
Self-Assessment.

CRITERION #5: IMPROVE:

In my belief, the answer to this
question is clearly defined:

5 Strongly Agree

4 Agree

3 Neutral

2 Disagree

1 Strongly Disagree

1. What criteria will you use to assess your data
science team risks?
<--- Score

2. Is data science team documentation maintained?
<--- Score

3. What are your current levels and trends in key
measures or indicators of workforce and leader

development?
<--- Score

4. Are the most efficient solutions problem-specific?
<--- Score

5. Who are the people involved in developing and implementing data science team?
<--- Score

6. What tools were used to tap into the creativity and encourage 'outside the box' thinking?
<--- Score

7. Can you integrate quality management and risk management?
<--- Score

8. Do the viable solutions scale to future needs?
<--- Score

9. What are the expected data science team results?
<--- Score

10. data science team risk decisions: whose call Is It?
<--- Score

11. How is knowledge sharing about risk management improved?
<--- Score

12. How do you improve data science team service perception, and satisfaction?
<--- Score

13. What went well, what should change, what can

improve?
<--- Score

14. What improvements have been achieved?
<--- Score

15. Are the key business and technology risks being managed?
<--- Score

16. How significant is the improvement in the eyes of the end user?
<--- Score

17. What risks do you need to manage?
<--- Score

18. What needs improvement? Why?
<--- Score

19. Explorations of the frontiers of data science team will help you build influence, improve data science team, optimize decision making, and sustain change, what is your approach?
<--- Score

20. How do you go about comparing data science team approaches/solutions?
<--- Score

21. How can you improve performance?
<--- Score

22. What resources are required for the improvement efforts?
<--- Score

23. Who controls key decisions that will be made?
<--- Score

24. What can you do to improve?
<--- Score

25. What are the concrete data science team results?
<--- Score

26. What lessons, if any, from a pilot were incorporated into the design of the full-scale solution?
<--- Score

27. What tools were used to evaluate the potential solutions?
<--- Score

28. How will you know that a change is an improvement?
<--- Score

29. How do you improve your likelihood of success ?
<--- Score

30. Can the solution be designed and implemented within an acceptable time period?
<--- Score

31. How do you improve productivity?
<--- Score

32. Are risk management tasks balanced centrally and locally?
<--- Score

33. Do vendor agreements bring new compliance risk
?
<--- Score

34. Are decisions made in a timely manner?
<--- Score

35. Have you identified breakpoints and/or risk
tolerances that will trigger broad consideration of
a potential need for intervention or modification of
strategy?
<--- Score

36. What are the affordable data science team risks?
<--- Score

37. How is continuous improvement applied to risk
management?
<--- Score

38. How will you measure the results?
<--- Score

39. Are you assessing data science team and risk?
<--- Score

40. Do you cover the five essential competencies:
Communication, Collaboration,Innovation,
Adaptability, and Leadership that improve an
organizations ability to leverage the new data science
team in a volatile global economy?
<--- Score

41. Who do you report data science team results to?
<--- Score

42. Would you develop a data science team Communication Strategy?
<--- Score

43. Can you identify any significant risks or exposures to data science team third- parties (vendors, service providers, alliance partners etc) that concern you?
<--- Score

44. What area needs the greatest improvement?
<--- Score

45. How are policy decisions made and where?
<--- Score

46. What is the data science team's sustainability risk?
<--- Score

47. How will you recognize and celebrate results?
<--- Score

48. Which data science team solution is appropriate?
<--- Score

49. Risk Identification: What are the possible risk events your organization faces in relation to data science team?
<--- Score

50. How does your organization evaluate strategic data science team success?
<--- Score

51. What actually has to improve and by how much?
<--- Score

52. How do you deal with data science team risk?
<--- Score

53. How do you measure risk?
<--- Score

54. How do you keep improving data science team?
<--- Score

55. Was a data science team charter developed?
<--- Score

56. How will you know when its improved?
<--- Score

57. How do you manage data science team risk?
<--- Score

58. Is risk periodically assessed?
<--- Score

59. Who will be responsible for making the decisions
to include or exclude requested changes once data
science team is underway?
<--- Score

60. Is there any other data science team solution?
<--- Score

61. Who controls the risk?
<--- Score

62. How do you measure improved data science team
service perception, and satisfaction?
<--- Score

63. How do you manage and improve your data science team work systems to deliver customer value and achieve organizational success and sustainability?
<--- Score

64. How risky is your organization?
<--- Score

65. How can skill-level changes improve data science team?
<--- Score

66. How can you improve data science team?
<--- Score

67. What is the risk?
<--- Score

68. Risk factors: what are the characteristics of data science team that make it risky?
<--- Score

69. Risk events: what are the things that could go wrong?
<--- Score

70. Which of the recognised risks out of all risks can be most likely transferred?
<--- Score

71. What is the magnitude of the improvements?
<--- Score

72. Who manages data science team risk?
<--- Score

73. What current systems have to be understood and/or changed?
<--- Score

74. Who manages supplier risk management in your organization?
<--- Score

75. Does a good decision guarantee a good outcome?
<--- Score

76. Is any data science team documentation required?
<--- Score

77. Is the data science team solution sustainable?
<--- Score

78. Who makes the data science team decisions in your organization?
<--- Score

79. Have you achieved data science team improvements?
<--- Score

80. Is the scope clearly documented?
<--- Score

81. What practices helps your organization to develop its capacity to recognize patterns?
<--- Score

82. How can you better manage risk?
<--- Score

83. Do those selected for the data science team team

have a good general understanding of what data science team is all about?
<--- Score

84. Who will be responsible for documenting the data science team requirements in detail?
<--- Score

85. Who are the data science team decision-makers?
<--- Score

86. Who will be using the results of the measurement activities?
<--- Score

87. Do you need to do a usability evaluation?
<--- Score

88. Is the data science team documentation thorough?
<--- Score

89. What is the team's contingency plan for potential problems occurring in implementation?
<--- Score

90. For decision problems, how do you develop a decision statement?
<--- Score

91. How do you measure progress and evaluate training effectiveness?
<--- Score

92. Who should make the data science team decisions?

<--- Score

93. What is data science team risk?
<--- Score

94. In the past few months, what is the smallest change you have made that has had the biggest positive result? What was it about that small change that produced the large return?
<--- Score

95. What data science team improvements can be made?
<--- Score

96. If you could go back in time five years, what decision would you make differently? What is your best guess as to what decision you're making today you might regret five years from now?
<--- Score

97. Will the controls trigger any other risks?
<--- Score

98. What is data science team's impact on utilizing the best solution(s)?
<--- Score

99. For estimation problems, how do you develop an estimation statement?
<--- Score

100. At what point will vulnerability assessments be performed once data science team is put into production (e.g., ongoing Risk Management after implementation)?

<--- Score

101. What are the implications of the one critical data science team decision 10 minutes, 10 months, and 10 years from now?
<--- Score

102. How will you know that you have improved?
<--- Score

103. Is supporting data science team documentation required?
<--- Score

104. What tools were most useful during the improve phase?
<--- Score

105. How does the team improve its work?
<--- Score

106. When you map the key players in your own work and the types/domains of relationships with them, which relationships do you find easy and which challenging, and why?
<--- Score

107. What alternative responses are available to manage risk?
<--- Score

108. Are the risks fully understood, reasonable and manageable?
<--- Score

109. How do the data science team results compare

with the performance of your competitors and other organizations with similar offerings?
<--- Score

110. Are events managed to resolution?
<--- Score

111. How do you define the solutions' scope?
<--- Score

112. Who are the data science team decision makers?
<--- Score

113. What do you want to improve?
<--- Score

114. What were the underlying assumptions on the cost-benefit analysis?
<--- Score

115. Do you have the optimal project management team structure?
<--- Score

116. How do you mitigate data science team risk?
<--- Score

117. Is the measure of success for data science team understandable to a variety of people?
<--- Score

118. Is the solution technically practical?
<--- Score

119. How are data science team risks managed?
<--- Score

120. To what extent does management recognize data science team as a tool to increase the results?
<--- Score

121. Is the data science team risk managed?
<--- Score

122. Do you combine technical expertise with business knowledge and data science team Key topics include lifecycles, development approaches, requirements and how to make a business case?
<--- Score

123. What assumptions are made about the solution and approach?
<--- Score

124. Does the goal represent a desired result that can be measured?
<--- Score

125. How can the phases of data science team development be identified?
<--- Score

126. Are procedures documented for managing data science team risks?
<--- Score

127. What were the criteria for evaluating a data science team pilot?
<--- Score

128. Where do the data science team decisions reside?
<--- Score

129. Why improve in the first place?
<--- Score

130. What should a proof of concept or pilot accomplish?
<--- Score

131. What strategies for data science team improvement are successful?
<--- Score

132. What to do with the results or outcomes of measurements?
<--- Score

133. Where do you need data science team improvement?
<--- Score

134. What are the data science team security risks?
<--- Score

135. How do you link measurement and risk?
<--- Score

Add up total points for this section:
_ _ _ _ _ = Total points for this section

Divided by: _ _ _ _ _ _ (number of statements answered) = _ _ _ _ _ _
Average score for this section

Transfer your score to the data science team Index at the beginning of the Self-Assessment.

CRITERION #6: CONTROL:

INTENT: Implement the practical solution. Maintain the performance and correct possible complications.

In my belief, the answer to this question is clearly defined:

5 Strongly Agree

4 Agree

3 Neutral

2 Disagree

1 Strongly Disagree

1. Does job training on the documented procedures need to be part of the process team's education and training?
<--- Score

2. What should the next improvement project be that is related to data science team?
<--- Score

3. Will any special training be provided for results interpretation?
<--- Score

4. In the case of a data science team project, the criteria for the audit derive from implementation objectives, an audit of a data science team project involves assessing whether the recommendations outlined for implementation have been met, can you track that any data science team project is implemented as planned, and is it working?
<--- Score

5. How do you spread information?
<--- Score

6. Is a response plan in place for when the input, process, or output measures indicate an 'out-of-control' condition?
<--- Score

7. How will the process owner verify improvement in present and future sigma levels, process capabilities?
<--- Score

8. How is change control managed?
<--- Score

9. What is the best design framework for data science team organization now that, in a post industrial-age if the top-down, command and control model is no longer relevant?
<--- Score

10. What is your theory of human motivation, and how does your compensation plan fit with that view?

<--- Score

11. How is data science team project cost planned, managed, monitored?
<--- Score

12. Is there documentation that will support the successful operation of the improvement?
<--- Score

13. How widespread is its use?
<--- Score

14. How do you plan for the cost of succession?
<--- Score

15. Are new process steps, standards, and documentation ingrained into normal operations?
<--- Score

16. Are the planned controls working?
<--- Score

17. How do you encourage people to take control and responsibility?
<--- Score

18. Act/Adjust: What Do you Need to Do Differently?
<--- Score

19. Who will be in control?
<--- Score

20. Does the response plan contain a definite closed loop continual improvement scheme (e.g., plan-do-check-act)?

<--- Score

21. What is the control/monitoring plan?
<--- Score

22. Are operating procedures consistent?
<--- Score

23. Do data science teams have standardized and repeatable processes for executing analytical workflows that are documented and shared across teams?
<--- Score

24. What are your results for key measures or indicators of the accomplishment of your data science team strategy and action plans, including building and strengthening core competencies?
<--- Score

25. Is there a recommended audit plan for routine surveillance inspections of data science team's gains?
<--- Score

26. Against what alternative is success being measured?
<--- Score

27. How do you select, collect, align, and integrate data science team data and information for tracking daily operations and overall organizational performance, including progress relative to strategic objectives and action plans?
<--- Score

28. Can support from partners be adjusted?

<--- Score

29. Are you measuring, monitoring and predicting data science team activities to optimize operations and profitability, and enhancing outcomes?
<--- Score

30. Will the team be available to assist members in planning investigations?
<--- Score

31. Are documented procedures clear and easy to follow for the operators?
<--- Score

32. Does a troubleshooting guide exist or is it needed?
<--- Score

33. You may have created your quality measures at a time when you lacked resources, technology wasn't up to the required standard, or low service levels were the industry norm. Have those circumstances changed?
<--- Score

34. What do you stand for--and what are you against?
<--- Score

35. What can you control?
<--- Score

36. Has the improved process and its steps been standardized?
<--- Score

37. Will existing staff require re-training, for example,

to learn new business processes?
<--- Score

38. What is the standard for acceptable data science team performance?
<--- Score

39. What are the critical parameters to watch?
<--- Score

40. Can you adapt and adjust to changing data science team situations?
<--- Score

41. How will data science team decisions be made and monitored?
<--- Score

42. Is a response plan established and deployed?
<--- Score

43. How will the day-to-day responsibilities for monitoring and continual improvement be transferred from the improvement team to the process owner?
<--- Score

44. Are controls in place and consistently applied?
<--- Score

45. What adjustments to the strategies are needed?
<--- Score

46. How likely is the current data science team plan to come in on schedule or on budget?
<--- Score

47. Do you monitor the data science team decisions made and fine tune them as they evolve?
<--- Score

48. What is your plan to assess your security risks?
<--- Score

49. What are customers monitoring?
<--- Score

50. Is knowledge gained on process shared and institutionalized?
<--- Score

51. Are there documented procedures?
<--- Score

52. Who is going to spread your message?
<--- Score

53. Is there a documented and implemented monitoring plan?
<--- Score

54. How do senior leaders actions reflect a commitment to the organizations data science team values?
<--- Score

55. What other areas of the group might benefit from the data science team team's improvements, knowledge, and learning?
<--- Score

56. How will the process owner and team be able to

hold the gains?
<--- Score

57. How do you plan on providing proper recognition and disclosure of supporting companies?
<--- Score

58. How will report readings be checked to effectively monitor performance?
<--- Score

59. Does data science team appropriately measure and monitor risk?
<--- Score

60. How can you best use all of your knowledge repositories to enhance learning and sharing?
<--- Score

61. Is there an action plan in case of emergencies?
<--- Score

62. How will you measure your QA plan's effectiveness?
<--- Score

63. How do your controls stack up?
<--- Score

64. Is new knowledge gained imbedded in the response plan?
<--- Score

65. What data science team standards are applicable?
<--- Score

66. What should you measure to verify efficiency gains?
<--- Score

67. Is there a control plan in place for sustaining improvements (short and long-term)?
<--- Score

68. How might the group capture best practices and lessons learned so as to leverage improvements?
<--- Score

69. Do the data science team decisions you make today help people and the planet tomorrow?
<--- Score

70. Are pertinent alerts monitored, analyzed and distributed to appropriate personnel?
<--- Score

71. Who controls critical resources?
<--- Score

72. What is the recommended frequency of auditing?
<--- Score

73. What key inputs and outputs are being measured on an ongoing basis?
<--- Score

74. Implementation Planning: is a pilot needed to test the changes before a full roll out occurs?
<--- Score

75. What are the known security controls?
<--- Score

76. Do you monitor the effectiveness of your data science team activities?
<--- Score

77. Has the data science team value of standards been quantified?
<--- Score

78. What other systems, operations, processes, and infrastructures (hiring practices, staffing, training, incentives/rewards, metrics/dashboards/scorecards, etc.) need updates, additions, changes, or deletions in order to facilitate knowledge transfer and improvements?
<--- Score

79. Who has control over resources?
<--- Score

80. How will new or emerging customer needs/requirements be checked/communicated to orient the process toward meeting the new specifications and continually reducing variation?
<--- Score

81. Is reporting being used or needed?
<--- Score

82. Is there a transfer of ownership and knowledge to process owner and process team tasked with the responsibilities.
<--- Score

83. Does the data science team performance meet the customer's requirements?

<--- Score

84. Is there a standardized process?
<--- Score

85. Are the planned controls in place?
<--- Score

86. Are the data science team standards challenging?
<--- Score

87. What are the key elements of your data science team performance improvement system, including your evaluation, organizational learning, and innovation processes?
<--- Score

88. What are you attempting to measure/monitor?
<--- Score

89. Who is the data science team process owner?
<--- Score

90. Will your goals reflect your program budget?
<--- Score

91. How will input, process, and output variables be checked to detect for sub-optimal conditions?
<--- Score

92. Are suggested corrective/restorative actions indicated on the response plan for known causes to problems that might surface?
<--- Score

93. What do you measure to verify effectiveness

gains?
<--- Score

94. What quality tools were useful in the control phase?
<--- Score

95. How do controls support value?
<--- Score

96. Who sets the data science team standards?
<--- Score

97. Have new or revised work instructions resulted?
<--- Score

98. Is there a data science team Communication plan covering who needs to get what information when?
<--- Score

Add up total points for this section:
_ _ _ _ _ = Total points for this section

Divided by: _ _ _ _ _ _ (number of statements answered) = _ _ _ _ _ _
Average score for this section

Transfer your score to the data science team Index at the beginning of the Self-Assessment.

CRITERION #7: SUSTAIN:

INTENT: Retain the benefits.

In my belief, the answer to this question is clearly defined:

5 Strongly Agree

4 Agree

3 Neutral

2 Disagree

1 Strongly Disagree

1. Who is responsible for data science team?
<--- Score

2. How do you assess the data science team pitfalls that are inherent in implementing it?
<--- Score

3. Who is responsible for errors?
<--- Score

4. How do you stay inspired?

<--- Score

5. If you had to rebuild your organization without any traditional competitive advantages (i.e., no killer technology, promising research, innovative product/ service delivery model, etcetera), how would your people have to approach their work and collaborate together in order to create the necessary conditions for success?
<--- Score

6. How do you deal with data science team changes?
<--- Score

7. What are current data science team paradigms?
<--- Score

8. What is your competitive advantage?
<--- Score

9. What are the long-term data science team goals?
<--- Score

10. Why do and why don't your customers like your organization?
<--- Score

11. Is data science team dependent on the successful delivery of a current project?
<--- Score

12. What must you excel at?
<--- Score

13. How do you create buy-in?
<--- Score

14. Which functions and people interact with the supplier and or customer?
<--- Score

15. What are the challenges?
<--- Score

16. How do you go about securing data science team?
<--- Score

17. Who are four people whose careers you have enhanced?
<--- Score

18. What projects are going on in the organization today, and what resources are those projects using from the resource pools?
<--- Score

19. Can you maintain your growth without detracting from the factors that have contributed to your success?
<--- Score

20. How long will it take to change?
<--- Score

21. How do you set data science team stretch targets and how do you get people to not only participate in setting these stretch targets but also that they strive to achieve these?
<--- Score

22. What management system can you use to leverage the data science team experience, ideas,

and concerns of the people closest to the work to be done?
<--- Score

23. Are you changing as fast as the world around you?
<--- Score

24. Do you think data science team accomplishes the goals you expect it to accomplish?
<--- Score

25. Who uses your product in ways you never expected?
<--- Score

26. What stupid rule would you most like to kill?
<--- Score

27. Who will determine interim and final deadlines?
<--- Score

28. Instead of going to current contacts for new ideas, what if you reconnected with dormant contacts-- the people you used to know? If you were going reactivate a dormant tie, who would it be?
<--- Score

29. If you weren't already in this business, would you enter it today? And if not, what are you going to do about it?
<--- Score

30. Are you paying enough attention to the partners your company depends on to succeed?
<--- Score

31. Is the data science team organization completing tasks effectively and efficiently?
<--- Score

32. What happens at your organization when people fail?
<--- Score

33. How do you proactively clarify deliverables and data science team quality expectations?
<--- Score

34. Is the impact that data science team has shown?
<--- Score

35. What would have to be true for the option on the table to be the best possible choice?
<--- Score

36. Are you / should you be revolutionary or evolutionary?
<--- Score

37. What potential megatrends could make your business model obsolete?
<--- Score

38. Why is it important to have senior management support for a data science team project?
<--- Score

39. What is your data science team strategy?
<--- Score

40. What information is critical to your organization that your executives are ignoring?

<--- Score

41. What happens when a new employee joins the organization?
<--- Score

42. What are specific data science team rules to follow?
<--- Score

43. What is the overall business strategy?
<--- Score

44. If your customer were your grandmother, would you tell her to buy what you're selling?
<--- Score

45. What are the business goals data science team is aiming to achieve?
<--- Score

46. Are you maintaining a past–present–future perspective throughout the data science team discussion?
<--- Score

47. What is your question? Why?
<--- Score

48. What trophy do you want on your mantle?
<--- Score

49. If no one would ever find out about your accomplishments, how would you lead differently?
<--- Score

50. What is the range of capabilities?
<--- Score

51. What are strategies for increasing support and reducing opposition?
<--- Score

52. Why is data science team important for you now?
<--- Score

53. What knowledge, skills and characteristics mark a good data science team project manager?
<--- Score

54. Operational - will it work?
<--- Score

55. Is maximizing data science team protection the same as minimizing data science team loss?
<--- Score

56. Which data science team goals are the most important?
<--- Score

57. How do customers see your organization?
<--- Score

58. How do you know if you are successful?
<--- Score

59. Political -is anyone trying to undermine this project?
<--- Score

60. At what moment would you think; Will I get fired?

<--- Score

61. Who, on the executive team or the board, has spoken to a customer recently?
<--- Score

62. How is implementation research currently incorporated into each of your goals?
<--- Score

63. Do data science team rules make a reasonable demand on a users capabilities?
<--- Score

64. Have benefits been optimized with all key stakeholders?
<--- Score

65. How do you make it meaningful in connecting data science team with what users do day-to-day?
<--- Score

66. What are the potential basics of data science team fraud?
<--- Score

67. Do you know who is a friend or a foe?
<--- Score

68. Are the assumptions believable and achievable?
<--- Score

69. What is the purpose of data science team in relation to the mission?
<--- Score

70. Who else should you help?
<--- Score

71. Are the criteria for selecting recommendations stated?
<--- Score

72. What may be the consequences for the performance of an organization if all stakeholders are not consulted regarding data science team?
<--- Score

73. What should you stop doing?
<--- Score

74. Can the schedule be done in the given time?
<--- Score

75. What is something you believe that nearly no one agrees with you on?
<--- Score

76. How will you insure seamless interoperability of data science team moving forward?
<--- Score

77. What tools do you use once you have decided on a data science team strategy and more importantly how do you choose?
<--- Score

78. If you got fired and a new hire took your place, what would she do different?
<--- Score

79. Can you break it down?

<--- Score

80. How do you manage data science team Knowledge Management (KM)?
<--- Score

81. How do you maintain data science team's Integrity?
<--- Score

82. How do you transition from the baseline to the target?
<--- Score

83. Is your strategy driving your strategy? Or is the way in which you allocate resources driving your strategy?
<--- Score

84. Who do we want your customers to become?
<--- Score

85. How likely is it that a customer would recommend your company to a friend or colleague?
<--- Score

86. What you are going to do to affect the numbers?
<--- Score

87. How much does data science team help?
<--- Score

88. Is there any reason to believe the opposite of my current belief?
<--- Score

89. How do you foster the skills, knowledge, talents, attributes, and characteristics you want to have?
<--- Score

90. What are internal and external data science team relations?
<--- Score

91. Are you satisfied with your current role? If not, what is missing from it?
<--- Score

92. Who will provide the final approval of data science team deliverables?
<--- Score

93. What is the craziest thing you can do?
<--- Score

94. What role does communication play in the success or failure of a data science team project?
<--- Score

95. Is data science team realistic, or are you setting yourself up for failure?
<--- Score

96. What new services of functionality will be implemented next with data science team ?
<--- Score

97. How will you motivate the stakeholders with the least vested interest?
<--- Score

98. What is the source of the strategies for data

science team strengthening and reform?
<--- Score

99. How do you provide a safe environment
-physically and emotionally?
<--- Score

100. Is your basic point _____ or _____?
<--- Score

101. If you find that you havent accomplished one of
the goals for one of the steps of the data science team
strategy, what will you do to fix it?
<--- Score

102. What is an unauthorized commitment?
<--- Score

103. Were lessons learned captured and
communicated?
<--- Score

104. What have you done to protect your business
from competitive encroachment?
<--- Score

105. How can you incorporate support to ensure
safe and effective use of data science team into the
services that you provide?
<--- Score

106. How do you accomplish your long range data
science team goals?
<--- Score

107. Do you think you know, or do you know you

know ?
<--- Score

108. What is the kind of project structure that would be appropriate for your data science team project, should it be formal and complex, or can it be less formal and relatively simple?
<--- Score

109. In a project to restructure data science team outcomes, which stakeholders would you involve?
<--- Score

110. What are your personal philosophies regarding data science team and how do they influence your work?
<--- Score

111. How can you become more high-tech but still be high touch?
<--- Score

112. Do you have past data science team successes?
<--- Score

113. Are there any activities that you can take off your to do list?
<--- Score

114. What unique value proposition (UVP) do you offer?
<--- Score

115. Where can you break convention?
<--- Score

116. Will there be any necessary staff changes (redundancies or new hires)?
<--- Score

117. What are the gaps in your knowledge and experience?
<--- Score

118. How do you govern and fulfill your societal responsibilities?
<--- Score

119. How do senior leaders deploy your organizations vision and values through your leadership system, to the workforce, to key suppliers and partners, and to customers and other stakeholders, as appropriate?
<--- Score

120. Do you say no to customers for no reason?
<--- Score

121. Have new benefits been realized?
<--- Score

122. When information truly is ubiquitous, when reach and connectivity are completely global, when computing resources are infinite, and when a whole new set of impossibilities are not only possible, but happening, what will that do to your business?
<--- Score

123. Is a data science team breakthrough on the horizon?
<--- Score

124. What did you miss in the interview for the worst

hire you ever made?
<--- Score

125. What do we do when new problems arise?
<--- Score

126. Is there a work around that you can use?
<--- Score

127. Do you know what you are doing? And who do you call if you don't?
<--- Score

128. Do you have enough freaky customers in your portfolio pushing you to the limit day in and day out?
<--- Score

129. How can you negotiate data science team successfully with a stubborn boss, an irate client, or a deceitful coworker?
<--- Score

130. What is the recommended frequency of auditing?
<--- Score

131. What counts that you are not counting?
<--- Score

132. What is effective data science team?
<--- Score

133. Is there any existing data science team governance structure?
<--- Score

134. Which models, tools and techniques are

necessary?
<--- Score

135. Who do you want your customers to become?
<--- Score

136. What are the essentials of internal data science team management?
<--- Score

137. Who is the main stakeholder, with ultimate responsibility for driving data science team forward?
<--- Score

138. Do you have an implicit bias for capital investments over people investments?
<--- Score

139. Is it economical; do you have the time and money?
<--- Score

140. Marketing budgets are tighter, consumers are more skeptical, and social media has changed forever the way we talk about data science team, how do you gain traction?
<--- Score

141. What will be the consequences to the stakeholder (financial, reputation etc) if data science team does not go ahead or fails to deliver the objectives?
<--- Score

142. Do you see more potential in people than they do in themselves?

<--- Score

143. Whom among your colleagues do you trust, and for what?
<--- Score

144. What have been your experiences in defining long range data science team goals?
<--- Score

145. Do you have the right people on the bus?
<--- Score

146. What are the short and long-term data science team goals?
<--- Score

147. What are you trying to prove to yourself, and how might it be hijacking your life and business success?
<--- Score

148. Who are your customers?
<--- Score

149. Has implementation been effective in reaching specified objectives so far?
<--- Score

150. How do you cross-sell and up-sell your data science team success?
<--- Score

151. What goals did you miss?
<--- Score

152. What is your formula for success in data science

team ?
<--- Score

153. What relationships among data science team trends do you perceive?
<--- Score

154. What are the key enablers to make this data science team move?
<--- Score

155. What are your most important goals for the strategic data science team objectives?
<--- Score

156. How do you keep the momentum going?
<--- Score

157. Who is on the team?
<--- Score

158. What threat is data science team addressing?
<--- Score

159. What would you recommend your friend do if he/she were facing this dilemma?
<--- Score

160. Who will be responsible for deciding whether data science team goes ahead or not after the initial investigations?
<--- Score

161. Do you feel that more should be done in the data science team area?
<--- Score

162. In retrospect, of the projects that you pulled the plug on, what percent do you wish had been allowed to keep going, and what percent do you wish had ended earlier?
<--- Score

163. What could happen if you do not do it?
<--- Score

164. Why not do data science team?
<--- Score

165. What are the success criteria that will indicate that data science team objectives have been met and the benefits delivered?
<--- Score

166. Whose voice (department, ethnic group, women, older workers, etc) might you have missed hearing from in your company, and how might you amplify this voice to create positive momentum for your business?
<--- Score

167. What are you challenging?
<--- Score

168. Who are the key stakeholders?
<--- Score

169. What one word do you want to own in the minds of your customers, employees, and partners?
<--- Score

170. Are you relevant? Will you be relevant five years

from now? Ten?

<--- Score

171. If you were responsible for initiating and implementing major changes in your organization, what steps might you take to ensure acceptance of those changes?

<--- Score

172. Do you have the right capabilities and capacities?

<--- Score

173. What are the usability implications of data science team actions?

<--- Score

174. How do you listen to customers to obtain actionable information?

<--- Score

175. How do you lead with data science team in mind?

<--- Score

176. Can you do all this work?

<--- Score

177. Why should you adopt a data science team framework?

<--- Score

178. Think of your data science team project, what are the main functions?

<--- Score

179. What does your signature ensure?

<--- Score

180. How will you ensure you get what you expected?
<--- Score

181. Would you rather sell to knowledgeable and informed customers or to uninformed customers?
<--- Score

182. What data science team skills are most important?
<--- Score

183. What is the estimated value of the project?
<--- Score

184. What is your BATNA (best alternative to a negotiated agreement)?
<--- Score

185. How do you engage the workforce, in addition to satisfying them?
<--- Score

186. Are assumptions made in data science team stated explicitly?
<--- Score

187. Did your employees make progress today?
<--- Score

188. Are you using a design thinking approach and integrating Innovation, data science team Experience, and Brand Value?
<--- Score

189. How do you determine the key elements that affect data science team workforce satisfaction, how are these elements determined for different workforce groups and segments?
<--- Score

190. How will you know that the data science team project has been successful?
<--- Score

191. Which individuals, teams or departments will be involved in data science team?
<--- Score

192. If there were zero limitations, what would you do differently?
<--- Score

193. What are the barriers to increased data science team production?
<--- Score

194. How much contingency will be available in the budget?
<--- Score

195. What is the overall talent health of your organization as a whole at senior levels, and for each organization reporting to a member of the Senior Leadership Team?
<--- Score

196. How do you keep records, of what?
<--- Score

197. What is the big data science team idea?

<--- Score

198. How can you become the company that would put you out of business?
<--- Score

199. Are new benefits received and understood?
<--- Score

200. Who will manage the integration of tools?
<--- Score

201. If you had to leave your organization for a year and the only communication you could have with employees/colleagues was a single paragraph, what would you write?
<--- Score

202. How does data science team integrate with other stakeholder initiatives?
<--- Score

203. What happens if you do not have enough funding?
<--- Score

204. To whom do you add value?
<--- Score

205. What is it like to work for you?
<--- Score

206. What trouble can you get into?
<--- Score

207. What are the top 3 things at the forefront of your

data science team agendas for the next 3 years?
<--- Score

208. What was the last experiment you ran?
<--- Score

209. What is a feasible sequencing of reform initiatives over time?
<--- Score

210. What data science team modifications can you make work for you?
<--- Score

Add up total points for this section:
_ _ _ _ _ = Total points for this section

Divided by: _ _ _ _ _ _ (number of statements answered) = _ _ _ _ _ _
Average score for this section

Transfer your score to the data science team Index at the beginning of the Self-Assessment.

Data Science Team and Managing Projects, Criteria for Project Managers:

1.0 Initiating Process Group: Data Science Team

1. What areas were overlooked on this Data Science Team project?

2. When are the deliverables to be generated in each phase?

3. Measurable - are the targets measurable?

4. During which stage of Risk planning are risks prioritized based on probability and impact?

5. Do you know the Data Science Team projects goal, purpose and objectives?

6. Were decisions made in a timely manner?

7. What are the tools and techniques to be used in each phase?

8. When will the Data Science Team project be done?

9. What are the required resources?

10. First of all, should any action be taken?

11. Who is performing the work of the Data Science Team project?

12. Do you understand the communication expectations for this Data Science Team project?

13. What input will you be required to provide the

Data Science Team project team?

14. Does it make any difference if you am successful?

15. Do you know if the Data Science Team project requires outside equipment or vendor resources?

16. Although the Data Science Team project manager does not directly manage procurement and contracting activities, who does manage procurement and contracting activities in your organization then if not the PM?

17. Are stakeholders properly informed about the status of the Data Science Team project?

18. When must it be done?

19. How can you make your needs known?

20. How to control and approve each phase?

1.1 Project Charter: Data Science Team

21. Is it an improvement over existing products?

22. When?

23. Pop quiz – which are the same inputs as in the Data Science Team project charter?

24. What is the business need?

25. When do you use a Data Science Team project Charter?

26. What are some examples of a business case?

27. What is the purpose of the Data Science Team project?

28. What material?

29. What is the most common tool for helping define the detail?

30. Assumptions and constraints: what assumptions were made in defining the Data Science Team project?

31. Market – identify products market, including whether it is outside of the objective: what is the purpose of the program or Data Science Team project?

32. Who is the Data Science Team project Manager?

33. Assumptions: what factors, for planning purposes, are you considering to be true?

34. Who manages integration?

35. Are there special technology requirements?

36. What are the assigned resources?

37. What is the justification?

38. Review the general mission What system will be affected by the improvement efforts?

39. What are the assumptions?

40. Major high-level milestone targets: what events measure progress?

1.2 Stakeholder Register: Data Science Team

41. What is the power of the stakeholder?

42. How much influence do they have on the Data Science Team project?

43. What & Why?

44. How should employers make voices heard?

45. Who are the stakeholders?

46. Who wants to talk about Security?

47. How will reports be created?

48. What are the major Data Science Team project milestones requiring communications or providing communications opportunities?

49. Is your organization ready for change?

50. How big is the gap?

51. Who is managing stakeholder engagement?

52. What opportunities exist to provide communications?

1.3 Stakeholder Analysis Matrix: Data Science Team

53. Innovative aspects?

54. What is the stakeholders name, what is function?

55. How does the Data Science Team project involve consultations or collaboration with other organizations?

56. If you can not fix it, how do you do it differently?

57. Political effects?

58. Why do you care?

59. Who are potential allies and opponents?

60. Information and research?

61. Seasonality, weather effects?

62. Benefit to whom?

63. How can you fill the need to show progress?

64. Usps (unique selling points)?

65. Inoculations or payment to receive them?

66. Cashflow, start-up cash-drain?

67. Marketing - reach, distribution, awareness?

68. New markets, vertical, horizontal?

69. Reputation, presence and reach?

70. What do your organizations stakeholders do better than anyone else?

71. What are the key services, contractual arrangements, or other relationships between stakeholder groups?

72. Which conditions out of the control of the management are crucial for the achievement of the immediate objective?

2.0 Planning Process Group: Data Science Team

73. How do you integrate Data Science Team project Planning with the Iterative/Evolutionary SDLC?

74. What factors are contributing to progress or delay in the achievement of products and results?

75. Is the pace of implementing the products of the program ensuring the completeness of the results of the Data Science Team project?

76. Are there efficient coordination mechanisms to avoid overloading the counterparts, participating stakeholders?

77. How well do the team follow the chosen processes?

78. How are the principles of aid effectiveness (ownership, alignment, management for development results and mutual responsibility) being applied in the Data Science Team project?

79. You did your readings, yes?

80. What is the difference between the early schedule and late schedule?

81. Are the follow-up indicators relevant and do they meet the quality needed to measure the outputs and outcomes of the Data Science Team project?

82. Why is it important to determine activity sequencing on Data Science Team projects?

83. Does the program have follow-up mechanisms (to verify the quality of the products, punctuality of delivery, etc.) to measure progress in the achievement of the envisaged results?

84. Contingency planning. if a risk event occurs, what will you do?

85. Data Science Team project assessment; why did you do this Data Science Team project?

86. Explanation: is what the Data Science Team project intents to solve a hard question?

87. What types of differentiated effects are resulting from the Data Science Team project and to what extent?

88. On which process should team members spend the most time?

89. If action is called for, what form should it take?

90. To what extent has the intervention strategy been adapted to the areas of intervention in which it is being implemented?

2.1 Project Management Plan: Data Science Team

91. What went right?

92. Why do you manage integration?

93. Is mitigation authorized or recommended?

94. Are the existing and future without-plan conditions reasonable and appropriate?

95. What would you do differently?

96. What is risk management?

97. When is the Data Science Team project management plan created?

98. Was the peer (technical) review of the cost estimates duly coordinated with the cost estimate center of expertise and addressed in the review documentation and certification?

99. Are the proposed Data Science Team project purposes different than a previously authorized Data Science Team project?

100. What if, for example, the positive direction and vision of your organization causes expected trends to change resulting in greater need than expected?

101. Does the implementation plan have an

appropriate division of responsibilities?

102. What are the deliverables?

103. Who is the sponsor?

104. Is there anything you would now do differently on your Data Science Team project based on past experience?

105. Where does all this information come from?

106. Why Change?

107. Are cost risk analysis methods applied to develop contingencies for the estimated total Data Science Team project costs?

108. What happened during the process that you found interesting?

109. Has the selected plan been formulated using cost effectiveness and incremental analysis techniques?

2.2 Scope Management Plan: Data Science Team

110. What happens to rejected deliverables?

111. Cost / benefit analysis?

112. Have external dependencies been captured in the schedule?

113. Are meeting objectives identified for each meeting?

114. Are funding resource estimates sufficiently detailed and documented for use in planning and tracking the Data Science Team project?

115. Has the schedule been baselined?

116. Are schedule deliverables actually delivered?

117. Are estimating assumptions and constraints captured?

118. What threats might prevent you from getting there?

119. Describe how the deliverables will be verified against the Data Science Team project scope. To whom will the deliverables be first presented for inspection and verification?

120. What should you drop in order to add something

new?

121. Are assumptions being identified, recorded, analyzed, qualified and closed?

122. Who is responsible for monitoring the Data Science Team project scope to ensure the Data Science Team project remains within the scope baseline?

123. Describe the manner in which Data Science Team project deliverables will be formally presented and accepted. Will they be presented at the end of each phase?

124. Are you spending the right amount of money for specific tasks?

125. Quality standards - are controls in place to ensure that the work was not only completed and also completed to meet specific standards?

126. Has a Data Science Team project Communications Plan been developed?

127. Can each item be appropriately scheduled?

128. Are risk oriented checklists used during risk identification?

2.3 Requirements Management Plan: Data Science Team

129. Controlling Data Science Team project requirements involves monitoring the status of the Data Science Team project requirements and managing changes to the requirements. Who is responsible for monitoring and tracking the Data Science Team project requirements?

130. How will you develop the schedule of requirements activities?

131. Who has the authority to reject Data Science Team project requirements?

132. Who is responsible for monitoring and tracking the Data Science Team project requirements?

133. How detailed should the Data Science Team project get?

134. Will you use an assessment of the Data Science Team project environment as a tool to discover risk to the requirements process?

135. Business analysis scope?

136. Why manage requirements?

137. After the requirements are gathered and set forth on the requirements register, theyre little more than a laundry list of items. Some may be duplicates,

some might conflict with others and some will be too broad or too vague to understand. Describe how the requirements will be analyzed. Who will perform the analysis?

138. If it exists, where is it housed?

139. Will the product release be stable and mature enough to be deployed in the user community?

140. What is the earliest finish date for this Data Science Team project if it is scheduled to start on ...?

141. Did you avoid subjective, flowery or non-specific statements?

142. How will requirements be managed?

143. Do you understand the role that each stakeholder will play in the requirements process?

144. Is the system software (non-operating system) new to the IT Data Science Team project team?

145. Who will approve the requirements (and if multiple approvers, in what order)?

146. Who is responsible for quantifying the Data Science Team project requirements?

147. Are actual resource expenditures versus planned still acceptable?

148. Are actual resources expenditures versus planned expenditures acceptable?

2.4 Requirements Documentation: Data Science Team

149. Has requirements gathering uncovered information that would necessitate changes?

150. Is the origin of the requirement clearly stated?

151. What happens when requirements are wrong?

152. Where do you define what is a customer, what are the attributes of customer?

153. How do you know when a Requirement is accurate enough?

154. Consistency. are there any requirements conflicts?

155. How will the proposed Data Science Team project help?

156. Who provides requirements?

157. How do you get the user to tell you what they want?

158. What images does it conjure?

159. Verifiability. can the requirements be checked?

160. How will they be documented / shared?

161. Basic work/business process; high-level, what is being touched?

162. What is effective documentation?

163. What are the attributes of a customer?

164. What facilities must be supported by the system?

165. Who is interacting with the system?

166. What will be the integration problems?

167. Is your business case still valid?

168. Validity. does the system provide the functions which best support the customers needs?

2.5 Requirements Traceability Matrix: Data Science Team

169. What is the WBS?

170. Do you have a clear understanding of all subcontracts in place?

171. Will you use a Requirements Traceability Matrix?

172. How will it affect the stakeholders personally in career?

173. Why do you manage scope?

174. What percentage of Data Science Team projects are producing traceability matrices between requirements and other work products?

175. Why use a WBS?

176. Is there a requirements traceability process in place?

177. Describe the process for approving requirements so they can be added to the traceability matrix and Data Science Team project work can be performed. Will the Data Science Team project requirements become approved in writing?

178. What are the chronologies, contingencies, consequences, criteria?

179. How small is small enough?

180. How do you manage scope?

2.6 Project Scope Statement: Data Science Team

181. Change management vs. change leadership - what is the difference?

182. Will all Data Science Team project issues be unconditionally tracked through the issue resolution process?

183. What is the product of this Data Science Team project?

184. Write a brief purpose statement for this Data Science Team project. Include a business justification statement. What is the product of this Data Science Team project?

185. Elements that deal with providing the detail?

186. Will the Data Science Team project risks be managed according to the Data Science Team projects risk management process?

187. What process would you recommend for creating the Data Science Team project scope statement?

188. Has the format for tracking and monitoring schedules and costs been defined?

189. Will all tasks resulting from issues be entered into the Data Science Team project Plan and tracked through the plan?

190. Have the reports to be produced, distributed, and filed been defined?

191. What are the defined meeting materials?

192. Will there be a Change Control Process in place?

193. What is change?

194. Has a method and process for requirement tracking been developed?

195. Has the Data Science Team project scope statement been reviewed as part of the baseline process?

196. Is an issue management process documented and filed?

197. Is the change control process documented and on file?

198. Is the Data Science Team project sponsor function identified and defined?

2.7 Assumption and Constraint Log: Data Science Team

199. No superfluous information or marketing narrative?

200. Do you know what your customers expectations are regarding this process?

201. Model-building: what data-analytic strategies are useful when building proportional-hazards models?

202. Was the document/deliverable developed per the appropriate or required standards (for example, Institute of Electrical and Electronics Engineers standards)?

203. Contradictory information between different documents?

204. Are there cosmetic errors that hinder readability and comprehension?

205. Is there documentation of system capability requirements, data requirements, environment requirements, security requirements, and computer and hardware requirements?

206. What worked well?

207. What weaknesses do you have?

208. What strengths do you have?

209. What to do at recovery?

210. Are you meeting your customers expectations consistently?

211. Does a documented Data Science Team project organizational policy & plan (i.e. governance model) exist?

212. What other teams / processes would be impacted by changes to the current process, and how?

213. Have the scope, objectives, costs, benefits and impacts been communicated to all involved and/or impacted stakeholders and work groups?

214. Have you eliminated all duplicative tasks or manual efforts, where appropriate?

215. Does the traceability documentation describe the tool and/or mechanism to be used to capture traceability throughout the life cycle?

216. Are there ways to reduce the time it takes to get something approved?

217. Violation trace: why ?

2.8 Work Breakdown Structure: Data Science Team

218. When do you stop?

219. Is it a change in scope?

220. What has to be done?

221. How will you and your Data Science Team project team define the Data Science Team projects scope and work breakdown structure?

222. When does it have to be done?

223. When would you develop a Work Breakdown Structure?

224. Why is it useful?

225. How many levels?

226. How much detail?

227. Who has to do it?

228. Is the work breakdown structure (wbs) defined and is the scope of the Data Science Team project clear with assigned deliverable owners?

229. How big is a work-package?

230. How far down?

231. What is the probability that the Data Science Team project duration will exceed xx weeks?

232. What is the probability of completing the Data Science Team project in less that xx days?

233. Where does it take place?

234. Why would you develop a Work Breakdown Structure?

2.9 WBS Dictionary: Data Science Team

235. Are the contractors estimates of costs at completion reconcilable with cost data reported to us?

236. All cwbs elements specified for external reporting?

237. Does the contractors system identify work accomplishment against the schedule plan?

238. Are records maintained to show full accountability for all material purchased for the contract, including the residual inventory?

239. Are overhead cost budgets established for each organization which has authority to incur overhead costs?

240. Authorization to proceed with all authorized work?

241. Do work packages consist of discrete tasks which are adequately described?

242. Are control accounts opened and closed based on the start and completion of work contained therein?

243. Budgets assigned to major functional organizations?

244. Incurrence of actual indirect costs in excess of budgets, by element of expense?

245. Are Data Science Team projected overhead costs in each pool and the associated direct costs used as the basis for establishing interim rates for allocating overhead to contracts?

246. Contractor financial periods; for example, annual?

247. Are records maintained to show how management reserves are used?

248. The total budget for the contract (including estimates for authorized and unpriced work)?

249. Does the cost accumulation system provide for summarization of indirect costs from the point of allocation to the contract total?

250. Is all contract work included in the CWBS?

251. Are internal budgets for authorized, and not priced changes based on the contractors resource plan for accomplishing the work?

252. Are data elements (BCWS, BCWP, and ACWP) progressively summarized from the detail level to the contract level through the CWBS?

253. Knowledgeable Data Science Team projections of future performance?

2.10 Schedule Management Plan: Data Science Team

254. What happens if a warning is triggered?

255. Are vendor contract reports, reviews and visits conducted periodically?

256. Are the key elements of a Data Science Team project Charter present?

257. Were the budget estimates reasonable?

258. Have reserves been created to address risks?

259. Are the constraints or deadlines associated with the task accurate?

260. Are staff skills known and available for each task?

261. Are there checklists created to determine if all quality processes are followed?

262. Do Data Science Team project teams & team members report on status / activities / progress?

263. Are procurement deliverables arriving on time and to specification?

264. Where is the scheduling tool and who has access to it to view it?

265. Are all activities logically sequenced?

266. Are the predecessor and successor relationships accurate?

267. Is a payment system in place with proper reviews and approvals?

268. Is the critical path valid?

269. Is quality monitored from the perspective of the customers needs and expectations?

270. Personnel with expertise?

2.11 Activity List: Data Science Team

271. How difficult will it be to do specific activities on this Data Science Team project?

272. What will be performed?

273. How much slack is available in the Data Science Team project?

274. Are the required resources available or need to be acquired?

275. What is the probability the Data Science Team project can be completed in xx weeks?

276. Is infrastructure setup part of your Data Science Team project?

277. What are you counting on?

278. What is the total time required to complete the Data Science Team project if no delays occur?

279. Where will it be performed?

280. What went wrong?

281. How do you determine the late start (LS) for each activity?

282. What did not go as well?

283. For other activities, how much delay can be

tolerated?

284. How can the Data Science Team project be displayed graphically to better visualize the activities?

285. The wbs is developed as part of a joint planning session. and how do you know that youhave done this right?

286. What is the LF and LS for each activity?

287. How should ongoing costs be monitored to try to keep the Data Science Team project within budget?

288. In what sequence?

289. What went well?

290. Is there anything planned that does not need to be here?

2.12 Activity Attributes: Data Science Team

291. Have you identified the Activity Leveling Priority code value on each activity?

292. What is your organizations history in doing similar activities?

293. Were there other ways you could have organized the data to achieve similar results?

294. What conclusions/generalizations can you draw from this?

295. Can more resources be added?

296. Activity: what is In the Bag?

297. What activity do you think you should spend the most time on?

298. Are the required resources available?

299. Time for overtime?

300. How much activity detail is required?

301. Has management defined a definite timeframe for the turnaround or Data Science Team project window?

302. Which method produces the more accurate cost

assignment?

303. How difficult will it be to do specific activities on this Data Science Team project?

304. Resources to accomplish the work?

305. What is missing?

2.13 Milestone List: Data Science Team

306. Describe the industry you are in and the market growth opportunities. What is the market for your technology, product or service?

307. Milestone pages should display the UserID of the person who added the milestone. Does a report or query exist that provides this audit information?

308. Identify critical paths (one or more) and which activities are on the critical path?

309. How do you manage time?

310. Sustaining internal capabilities?

311. Describe the concept of the technology, product or service that will be or has been developed. How will it be used?

312. Competitive advantages?

313. Reliability of data, plan predictability?

314. Vital contracts and partners?

315. How will you get the word out to customers?

316. What date will the task finish?

317. Obstacles faced?

318. How soon can the activity start?

319. How difficult will it be to do specific activities on this Data Science Team project?

320. It is to be a narrative text providing the crucial aspects of your Data Science Team project proposal answering what, who, how, when and where?

321. How late can each activity be finished and started?

322. What would happen if a delivery of material was one week late?

2.14 Network Diagram: Data Science Team

323. If x is long, what would be the completion time if you break x into two parallel parts of y weeks and z weeks?

324. Why must you schedule milestones, such as reviews, throughout the Data Science Team project?

325. What to do and When?

326. If the Data Science Team project network diagram cannot change and you have extra personnel resources, what is the BEST thing to do?

327. What can be done concurrently?

328. What job or jobs follow it?

329. What are the Key Success Factors?

330. What job or jobs precede it?

331. What activity must be completed immediately before this activity can start?

332. What activities must occur simultaneously with this activity?

333. Where do you schedule uncertainty time?

334. What controls the start and finish of a job?

335. What are the Major Administrative Issues?

336. Planning: who, how long, what to do?

337. Review the logical flow of the network diagram. Take a look at which activities you have first and then sequence the activities. Do they make sense?

338. Exercise: what is the probability that the Data Science Team project duration will exceed xx weeks?

339. What job or jobs could run concurrently?

340. What must be completed before an activity can be started?

341. Are you on time?

342. How confident can you be in your milestone dates and the delivery date?

2.15 Activity Resource Requirements: Data Science Team

343. Do you use tools like decomposition and rolling-wave planning to produce the activity list and other outputs?

344. Why do you do that?

345. When does monitoring begin?

346. Other support in specific areas?

347. What is the Work Plan Standard?

348. How many signatures do you require on a check and does this match what is in your policy and procedures?

349. How do you handle petty cash?

350. Organizational Applicability?

351. Anything else?

352. Which logical relationship does the PDM use most often?

353. What are constraints that you might find during the Human Resource Planning process?

354. Are there unresolved issues that need to be addressed?

2.16 Resource Breakdown Structure: Data Science Team

355. When do they need the information?

356. Why time management?

357. Who delivers the information?

358. Goals for the Data Science Team project. What is each stakeholders desired outcome for the Data Science Team project?

359. What are the requirements for resource data?

360. How difficult will it be to do specific activities on this Data Science Team project?

361. What is the primary purpose of the human resource plan?

362. Who will use the system?

363. Why do you do it?

364. Any changes from stakeholders?

365. What defines a successful Data Science Team project?

366. What is Data Science Team project communication management?

367. Who will be used as a Data Science Team project team member?

368. How should the information be delivered?

369. Which resources should be in the resource pool?

370. How can this help you with team building?

371. The list could probably go on, but, the thing that you would most like to know is, How long & How much?

2.17 Activity Duration Estimates: Data Science Team

372. Will new hardware or software be required for servers or client machines?

373. Briefly summarize the work done by Maslow, Herzberg, McClellan, McGregor, Ouchi, Thamhain and Wilemon, and Covey. How do theories relate to Data Science Team project management?

374. What do corresponding sources say about Data Science Team project management?

375. Describe a Data Science Team project that suffered from scope creep. Could it have been avoided?

376. Are Data Science Team project results verified and Data Science Team project documents archived?

377. What do you think the real problem was in this case?

378. What is the duration of a milestone?

379. Account for the make-or-buy process and how to perform the financial calculations involved in the process. What are the main types of contracts if you do decide to outsource?

380. Does a process exist to formally recognize new Data Science Team projects?

381. Is evaluation criteria defined to rate proposals?

382. Is a contract change control system defined to manage changes to contract terms and conditions?

383. Will the new application be developed using existing hardware, software, and networks?

384. Why is it difficult to use Data Science Team project management software well?

385. Does a process exist to identify which qualified resources may be attainable?

386. Are procurement documents used to solicit accurate and complete proposals from prospective sellers?

387. Do you agree with the suggestions provided for improving Data Science Team project communications?

388. How do functionality, system outputs, performance, reliability, and maintainability requirements affect quality planning?

389. Sigma Data Science Team project?

390. What are the advantages and disadvantages of PERT?

2.18 Duration Estimating Worksheet: Data Science Team

391. When, then?

392. What work will be included in the Data Science Team project?

393. Do any colleagues have experience with your organization and/or RFPs?

394. Is this operation cost effective?

395. Why estimate costs?

396. How should ongoing costs be monitored to try to keep the Data Science Team project within budget?

397. When do the individual activities need to start and finish?

398. Why estimate time and cost?

399. When does your organization expect to be able to complete it?

400. Can the Data Science Team project be constructed as planned?

401. What utility impacts are there?

402. Small or large Data Science Team project?

403. What is your role?

404. Will the Data Science Team project collaborate with the local community and leverage resources?

405. Done before proceeding with this activity or what can be done concurrently?

406. Is a construction detail attached (to aid in explanation)?

407. What info is needed?

2.19 Project Schedule: Data Science Team

408. Master Data Science Team project schedule?

409. Is the Data Science Team project schedule available for all Data Science Team project team members to review?

410. Are key risk mitigation strategies added to the Data Science Team project schedule?

411. What does that mean?

412. Was the Data Science Team project schedule reviewed by all stakeholders and formally accepted?

413. Should you include sub-activities?

414. To what degree is do you feel the entire team was committed to the Data Science Team project schedule?

415. Should you have a test for each code module?

416. Your best shot for providing estimations how complex/how much work does the activity require?

417. Is there a Schedule Management Plan that establishes the criteria and activities for developing, monitoring and controlling the Data Science Team project schedule?

418. How closely did the initial Data Science Team project Schedule compare with the actual schedule?

419. Verify that the update is accurate. Are all remaining durations correct?

420. Month Data Science Team project take?

421. How detailed should a Data Science Team project get?

422. Data Science Team project work estimates Who is managing the work estimate quality of work tasks in the Data Science Team project schedule?

423. Are activities connected because logic dictates the order in which others occur?

424. What documents, if any, will the subcontractor provide (eg Data Science Team project schedule, quality plan etc)?

2.20 Cost Management Plan: Data Science Team

425. Are corrective actions and variances reported?

426. Has the Data Science Team project manager been identified?

427. Are the quality tools and methods identified in the Quality Plan appropriate to the Data Science Team project?

428. Are the people assigned to the Data Science Team project sufficiently qualified?

429. Has a quality assurance plan been developed for the Data Science Team project?

430. Have all documents been archived in a Data Science Team project repository for each release?

431. Has the Data Science Team project scope been baselined?

432. Have all involved Data Science Team project stakeholders and work groups committed to the Data Science Team project?

433. Cost estimate preparation – What cost estimates will be prepared during the Data Science Team project phases?

434. Timeline and milestones?

435. Has your organization readiness assessment been conducted?

436. Why do you manage cost?

437. Are the key elements of a Data Science Team project Charter present?

438. Have adequate resources been provided by management to ensure Data Science Team project success?

439. Are decisions captured in a decisions log?

440. Are enough systems & user personnel assigned to the Data Science Team project?

441. Is there an approved case?

442. Schedule contingency – how will the schedule contingency be administrated?

443. Is pert / critical path or equivalent methodology being used?

2.21 Activity Cost Estimates: Data Science Team

444. How do you fund change orders?

445. Was it performed on time?

446. Who determines when the contractor is paid?

447. How many activities should you have?

448. Where can you get activity reports?

449. What makes a good activity description?

450. Are data needed on characteristics of care?

451. Will you need to provide essential services information about activities?

452. What were things that you need to improve?

453. How difficult will it be to do specific tasks on the Data Science Team project?

454. Review – what are some common errors in activities to avoid?

455. Were the tasks or work products prepared by the consultant useful?

456. What is included in indirect cost being allocated?

457. What skill level is required to do the job?

458. How do you allocate indirect costs to activities?

459. Estimated cost?

460. Certification of actual expenditures?

461. What is your organizations history in doing similar tasks?

462. Scope statement only direct or indirect costs as well?

2.22 Cost Estimating Worksheet: Data Science Team

463. What additional Data Science Team project(s) could be initiated as a result of this Data Science Team project?

464. Does the Data Science Team project provide innovative ways for stakeholders to overcome obstacles or deliver better outcomes?

465. What will others want?

466. What is the purpose of estimating?

467. Is it feasible to establish a control group arrangement?

468. What can be included?

469. Identify the timeframe necessary to monitor progress and collect data to determine how the selected measure has changed?

470. Is the Data Science Team project responsive to community need?

471. Can a trend be established from historical performance data on the selected measure and are the criteria for using trend analysis or forecasting methods met?

472. Value pocket identification & quantification what

are value pockets?

473. What costs are to be estimated?

474. What happens to any remaining funds not used?

475. Will the Data Science Team project collaborate with the local community and leverage resources?

476. How will the results be shared and to whom?

477. What is the estimated labor cost today based upon this information?

478. Who is best positioned to know and assist in identifying corresponding factors?

479. Ask: are others positioned to know, are others credible, and will others cooperate?

2.23 Cost Baseline: Data Science Team

480. How accurate do cost estimates need to be?

481. Are you meeting with your team regularly?

482. On budget?

483. Does it impact schedule, cost, quality?

484. Has the actual cost of the Data Science Team project (or Data Science Team project phase) been tallied and compared to the approved budget?

485. Is there anything you need from upper management in order to be successful?

486. Pcs for your new business. what would the life cycle costs be?

487. How long are you willing to wait before you find out were late?

488. How fast?

489. Has the Data Science Team project (or Data Science Team project phase) been evaluated against each objective established in the product description and Integrated Data Science Team project Plan?

490. If you sold 10x widgets on a day, what would the affect on profits be?

491. Data Science Team project goals -should others

be reconsidered?

492. Has the Data Science Team projected annual cost to operate and maintain the product(s) or service(s) been approved and funded?

493. Impact to environment?

494. Have all approved changes to the Data Science Team project requirement been identified and impact on the performance, cost, and schedule baselines documented?

495. Are you asking management for something as a result of this update?

2.24 Quality Management Plan: Data Science Team

496. Sampling part of task?

497. How do you ensure that your sampling methods and procedures meet your data quality objectives?

498. Are decisions/actions based on data collected?

499. Are there unnecessary steps that are creating bottlenecks and/or causing people to wait?

500. Is this a Requirement?

501. What is the Quality Management Plan?

502. What are the appropriate test methods to be used?

503. What is quality planning ?

504. Have adequate resources been provided by management to ensure Data Science Team project success?

505. Meet how often?

506. Was trending evident between audits?

507. Who gets results of work?

508. Are there nonconformance issues?

509. How do you decide what information to record?

510. Has a Data Science Team project Communications Plan been developed?

511. How are new requirements or changes to requirements identified?

512. How do you decide who is responsible for signing the data reports?

513. What procedures are used to determine if you use, and the number of split, replicate or duplicate samples taken at a site?

514. How does training support what is important to your organization and the individual?

2.25 Quality Metrics: Data Science Team

515. Has trace of defects been initiated?

516. Do you know how much profit a 10% decrease in waste would generate?

517. Are applicable standards referenced and available?

518. Is there alignment within your organization on definitions?

519. Are there any open risk issues?

520. What if the biggest risk to your business were the already stated people who do not complain?

521. Has risk analysis been adequately reviewed?

522. What method of measurement do you use?

523. Which are the right metrics to use?

524. Where is quality now?

525. Is a risk containment plan in place?

526. Who is willing to lead?

527. Which data do others need in one place to target areas of improvement?

528. Filter visualizations of interest?

529. What documentation is required?

530. Did the team meet the Data Science Team project success criteria documented in the Quality Metrics Matrix?

531. Is there a set of procedures to capture, analyze and act on quality metrics?

532. Are quality metrics defined?

533. Was review conducted per standard protocols?

534. Is quality culture a competitive advantage?

2.26 Process Improvement Plan: Data Science Team

535. Purpose of goal: the motive is determined by asking, why do you want to achieve this goal?

536. What lessons have you learned so far?

537. Are you making progress on the goals?

538. To elicit goal statements, do you ask a question such as, What do you want to achieve?

539. If a process improvement framework is being used, which elements will help the problems and goals listed?

540. Everyone agrees on what process improvement is, right?

541. Why quality management?

542. What is the return on investment?

543. Are you making progress on your improvement plan?

544. Has the time line required to move measurement results from the points of collection to databases or users been established?

545. Has a process guide to collect the data been developed?

546. Does explicit definition of the measures exist?

547. Does your process ensure quality?

548. What is the test-cycle concept?

549. Have the frequency of collection and the points in the process where measurements will be made been determined?

550. Are you making progress on the improvement framework?

551. Why do you want to achieve the goal?

552. Have the supporting tools been developed or acquired?

553. Have storage and access mechanisms and procedures been determined?

2.27 Responsibility Assignment Matrix: Data Science Team

554. Data Science Team projected economic escalation?

555. Cwbs elements to be subcontracted, with identification of subcontractors?

556. Does the scheduling system identify in a timely manner the status of work?

557. Contract line items and end items?

558. Who is responsible for work and budgets for each wbs?

559. No rs: if a task has no one listed as responsible, who is getting the job done?

560. What do people write/say on status/Data Science Team project reports?

561. The staff interests – is the group or the person interested in working for this Data Science Team project?

562. What do you do when people do not respond?

563. Does the accounting system provide a basis for auditing records of direct costs chargeable to the contract?

564. Changes in the nature of the overhead requirements?

565. What are the known stakeholder requirements?

566. Are the wbs and organizational levels for application of the Data Science Team projected overhead costs identified?

567. Does each role with Accountable responsibility have the authority within your organization to make the required decisions?

568. Will too many Signing-off responsibilities delay the completion of the activity/deliverable?

569. Are all elements of indirect expense identified to overhead cost budgets of Data Science Team projections?

570. What happens when others get pulled for higher priority Data Science Team projects?

571. Do you need to convince people that its well worth the time and effort?

2.28 Roles and Responsibilities: Data Science Team

572. Are the quality assurance functions and related roles and responsibilities clearly defined?

573. Who is responsible for implementation activities and where will the functions, roles and responsibilities be defined?

574. Are Data Science Team project team roles and responsibilities identified and documented?

575. Is feedback clearly communicated and non-judgmental?

576. Are your budgets supportive of a culture of quality data?

577. Have you ever been a part of this team?

578. What expectations were NOT met?

579. Attainable / achievable: the goal is attainable; can you actually accomplish the goal?

580. What expectations were met?

581. Who: who is involved?

582. How well did the Data Science Team project Team understand the expectations of specific roles and responsibilities?

583. What specific behaviors did you observe?

584. Are governance roles and responsibilities documented?

585. What should you do now to ensure that you are exceeding expectations and excelling in your current position?

586. What should you highlight for improvement?

587. Who is responsible for each task?

588. What should you do now to prepare for your career 5+ years from now?

589. What should you do now to ensure that you are meeting all expectations of your current position?

2.29 Human Resource Management Plan: Data Science Team

590. Has the scope management document been updated and distributed to help prevent scope creep?

591. Is the assigned Data Science Team project manager a PMP (Certified Data Science Team project manager) and experienced?

592. Do all stakeholders know how to access this repository and where to find the Data Science Team project documentation?

593. Are the results of quality assurance reviews provided to affected groups & individuals?

594. Are all key components of a Quality Assurance Plan present?

595. Responsiveness to change and the resulting demands for different skills and abilities?

596. How are superior performers differentiated from average performers?

597. Has a capability assessment been conducted?

598. Is there a formal process for updating the Data Science Team project baseline?

599. How to convince employees that this is a necessary process?

600. Has a structured approach been used to break work effort into manageable components (WBS)?

601. Are Data Science Team project contact logs kept up to date?

602. Are metrics used to evaluate and manage Vendors?

603. Is there a formal set of procedures supporting Issues Management?

604. What is the boss?

605. How will the Data Science Team project manage expectations & meet needs and requirements?

606. Are there dependencies with other initiatives or Data Science Team projects?

2.30 Communications Management Plan: Data Science Team

607. Do you feel more overwhelmed by stakeholders?

608. In your work, how much time is spent on stakeholder identification?

609. What data is going to be required?

610. Conflict resolution -which method when?

611. Can you think of other people who might have concerns or interests?

612. How often do you engage with stakeholders?

613. How much time does it take to do it?

614. What approaches do you use?

615. Do you have members of your team responsible for certain stakeholders?

616. What to know?

617. Why is stakeholder engagement important?

618. Who is the stakeholder?

619. Do you then often overlook a key stakeholder or stakeholder group?

620. What is the stakeholders level of authority?

621. Are there common objectives between the team and the stakeholder?

622. Who did you turn to if you had questions?

623. Are you constantly rushing from meeting to meeting?

624. Who were proponents/opponents?

2.31 Risk Management Plan: Data Science Team

625. What is the impact to the Data Science Team project if the item is not resolved in a timely fashion?

626. Risks should be identified during which phase of Data Science Team project management life cycle?

627. Which risks should get the attention?

628. Is the customer technically sophisticated in the product area?

629. Is Data Science Team project scope stable?

630. Are team members trained in the use of the tools?

631. Is a software Data Science Team project management tool available?

632. What did not work so well?

633. What would you do?

634. How is risk identification performed?

635. Financial risk -can your organization afford to undertake the Data Science Team project?

636. Who should be notified of the occurrence of each of the indicators?

637. Mitigation -how can you avoid the risk?

638. How can you fix it?

639. Is this an issue, action item, question or a risk?

640. Why might it be late?

641. Is the customer willing to commit significant time to the requirements gathering process?

642. Prioritized components/features?

643. Market risk -will the new service or product be useful to your organization or marketable to others?

644. Is there additional information that would make you more confident about your analysis?

2.32 Risk Register: Data Science Team

645. What are the main aims, objectives of the policy, strategy, or service and the intended outcomes?

646. Which key risks have ineffective responses or outstanding improvement actions?

647. Have other controls and solutions been implemented in other services which could be applied as an alternative to additional funding?

648. People risk -are people with appropriate skills available to help complete the Data Science Team project?

649. Cost/benefit – how much will the proposed mitigations cost and how does this cost compare with the potential cost of the risk event/situation should it occur?

650. Financial risk -can your organization afford to undertake the Data Science Team project?

651. Risk categories: what are the main categories of risks that should be addressed on this Data Science Team project?

652. Methodology: how will risk management be performed on this Data Science Team project?

653. What action, if any, has been taken to respond to the risk?

654. What should the audit role be in establishing a risk management process?

655. Can the likelihood and impact of failing to achieve corresponding recommendations and action plans be assessed?

656. How could corresponding Risk affect the Data Science Team project in terms of cost and schedule?

657. How is a Community Risk Register created?

658. Having taken action, how did the responses effect change, and where is the Data Science Team project now?

659. What is the probability and impact of the risk occurring?

660. What are the major risks facing the Data Science Team project?

661. Technology risk -is the Data Science Team project technically feasible?

662. What is the reason for current performance gaps and do the risks and opportunities identified previously account for this?

663. How are risks graded?

664. Preventative actions - planned actions to reduce the likelihood a risk will occur and/or reduce the seriousness should it occur. What should you do now?

2.33 Probability and Impact Assessment: Data Science Team

665. What are the probabilities of chosen technologies being suitable for local conditions?

666. Do you use any methods to analyze risks?

667. Can you avoid altogether some things that might go wrong?

668. Will new information become available during the Data Science Team project?

669. How do risks change during a Data Science Team project life cycle?

670. What are the likely future requirements?

671. What is the risk appetite?

672. Anticipated volatility of the requirements?

673. Are some people working on multiple Data Science Team projects?

674. What is the impact if the risk does occur?

675. How will economic events and trends likely affect the Data Science Team project?

676. Risk may be made during which step of risk management?

677. What are the industrial relations prevailing in your organization?

678. Have you worked with the customer in the past?

679. What risks are necessary to achieve success?

680. Is it necessary to deeply assess all Data Science Team project risks?

681. How much is the probability of a risk occurring?

682. Will there be an increase in the political conservatism?

2.34 Probability and Impact Matrix: Data Science Team

683. What are the current requirements of the customer?

684. How carefully have the potential competitors been identified?

685. Are flexibility and reuse paramount?

686. What is the industrial relations prevailing in this organization?

687. How completely has the customer been identified?

688. How is the risk management process used in practice?

689. Is Data Science Team project scope stable?

690. Which role do you have in the Data Science Team project?

691. What action would you take to the identified risks in the Data Science Team project?

692. Are the best people available?

693. What lifestyle shifts might occur in society?

694. Workarounds are determined during which risk

management process?

695. What would be the effect of slippage?

696. How do you analyze the risks in the different types of Data Science Team projects?

697. What needs to be DONE?

698. What is the culture of the market and your organization?

699. Do you train all developers in the process?

2.35 Risk Data Sheet: Data Science Team

700. What was measured?

701. What are you weak at and therefore need to do better?

702. What is the environment within which you operate (social trends, economic, community values, broad based participation, national directions etc.)?

703. Has a sensitivity analysis been carried out?

704. How reliable is the data source?

705. Will revised controls lead to tolerable risk levels?

706. What can happen?

707. How can hazards be reduced?

708. If it happens, what are the consequences?

709. Who has a vested interest in how you perform as your organization (our stakeholders)?

710. What are the main threats to your existence?

711. What are your core values?

712. Has the most cost-effective solution been chosen?

713. What do people affected think about the need for, and practicality of preventive measures?

714. Is the data sufficiently specified in terms of the type of failure being analyzed, and its frequency or probability?

715. Are new hazards created?

716. What are you trying to achieve (Objectives)?

717. Do effective diagnostic tests exist?

718. Potential for recurrence?

2.36 Procurement Management Plan: Data Science Team

719. Are Data Science Team project leaders committed to this Data Science Team project full time?

720. Was an original risk assessment/risk management plan completed?

721. Have key stakeholders been identified?

722. Are the schedule estimates reasonable given the Data Science Team project?

723. Were Data Science Team project team members involved in the development of activity & task decomposition?

724. Have Data Science Team project team accountabilities & responsibilities been clearly defined?

725. Are the payment terms being followed?

726. Pareto diagrams, statistical sampling, flow charting or trend analysis used quality monitoring?

727. What are you trying to accomplish?

728. Are post milestone Data Science Team project reviews (PMPR) conducted with your organization at least once a year?

729. Has the business need been clearly defined?

730. Does the resource management plan include a personnel development plan?

731. Are the quality tools and methods identified in the Quality Plan appropriate to the Data Science Team project?

732. Are Data Science Team project contact logs kept up to date?

733. Sensitivity analysis?

734. Is there a requirements change management processes in place?

2.37 Source Selection Criteria: Data Science Team

735. Do you want to have them collaborate at subfactor level?

736. How should the oral presentations be handled?

737. In the technical/management area, what criteria do you use to determine the final evaluation ratings?

738. With the rapid changes in information technology, will media be readable in five or ten years?

739. How much weight should be placed on past performance information?

740. Can you make a cost/technical tradeoff?

741. Can you identify proposed teaming partners and/or subcontractors and consider the nature and extent of proposed involvement in satisfying the Data Science Team project requirements?

742. How will you evaluate offerors proposals?

743. Who is on the Source Selection Advisory Committee?

744. What benefits are accrued from issuing a DRFP in advance of issuing a final RFP?

745. What documentation should be used to support the selection decision?

746. What common questions or problems are associated with debriefings?

747. How organization are proposed quotes/prices?

748. What information may not be provided?

749. How are oral presentations documented?

750. Who is entitled to a debriefing?

751. What documentation is needed for a tradeoff decision?

752. Comparison of each offers prices to the estimated prices -are there significant differences?

753. Do you prepare an independent cost estimate?

754. How should oral presentations be prepared for?

2.38 Stakeholder Management Plan: Data Science Team

755. Has a provision been made to reassess Data Science Team project risks at various Data Science Team project stages?

756. Have Data Science Team project management standards and procedures been identified / established and documented?

757. What methods are to be used for managing and monitoring subcontractors (eg agreements, contracts etc)?

758. What is the drawback in using qualitative Data Science Team project selection techniques?

759. Is a stakeholder management plan in place?

760. Is the Data Science Team project sponsor clearly communicating the business case or rationale for why this Data Science Team project is needed?

761. Are target dates established for each milestone deliverable?

762. Are the appropriate IT resources adequate to meet planned commitments?

763. Is stakeholder involvement adequate?

764. What is positive about the current process?

765. Are there standards for code development?

766. Are communication systems proposed compatible with staff skills and experience?

767. What conditions make using three-point estimating justifiable?

768. Which risks pose the highest threat?

769. Has a Data Science Team project Communications Plan been developed?

770. Are there checklists created to demine if all quality processes are followed?

771. Does the Data Science Team project have a Quality Culture?

772. Are meeting minutes captured and sent out after the meeting?

2.39 Change Management Plan: Data Science Team

773. Will you need new processes?

774. Who will do the training?

775. Has the training co-ordinator been provided with the training details and put in place the necessary arrangements?

776. Will the culture embrace or reject this change?

777. What are the current methods of sharing information and do there need to be new ones developed?

778. Is there a support model for this application and are the details available for distribution?

779. Do the proposed users have access to the appropriate documentation?

780. What risks may occur upfront?

781. Has the training provider been established?

782. Who might be able to help you the most?

783. What is the worst thing that can happen if you communicate information?

784. What are the training strategies?

785. How will the stakeholders share information and transfer knowledge?

786. Different application of an existing process?

787. Has the target training audience been identified and nominated?

788. Who is the audience for change management activities?

789. How can you best frame the message so that it addresses the audiences interests?

790. How far reaching in your organization is the change?

791. What tasks are needed?

792. What are the key change management success metrics?

3.0 Executing Process Group: Data Science Team

793. What is the product of your Data Science Team project?

794. What areas does the group agree are the biggest success on the Data Science Team project?

795. Based on your Data Science Team project communication management plan, what worked well?

796. What type of information goes in the quality assurance plan?

797. What are some crucial elements of a good Data Science Team project plan?

798. What are the critical steps involved with strategy mapping?

799. Will a new application be developed using existing hardware, software, and networks?

800. How well did the chosen processes fit the needs of the Data Science Team project?

801. How does Data Science Team project management relate to other disciplines?

802. Does the Data Science Team project team have enough people to execute the Data Science Team

project plan?

803. Would you rate yourself as being risk-averse, risk-neutral, or risk-seeking?

804. What is the difference between using brainstorming and the Delphi technique for risk identification?

805. How could stakeholders negatively impact your Data Science Team project?

806. What areas were overlooked on this Data Science Team project?

807. Do Data Science Team project managers understand your organizational context for Data Science Team projects?

808. Were sponsors and decision makers available when needed outside regularly scheduled meetings?

809. How well did the chosen processes produce the expected results?

810. How do you control progress of your Data Science Team project?

811. What are the critical steps involved in selecting measures and initiatives?

3.1 Team Member Status Report: Data Science Team

812. Is there evidence that staff is taking a more professional approach toward management of your organizations Data Science Team projects?

813. The problem with Reward & Recognition Programs is that the truly deserving people all too often get left out. How can you make it practical?

814. How it is to be done?

815. How much risk is involved?

816. When a teams productivity and success depend on collaboration and the efficient flow of information, what generally fails them?

817. Are the products of your organizations Data Science Team projects meeting customers objectives?

818. What is to be done?

819. How will resource planning be done?

820. Will the staff do training or is that done by a third party?

821. Does every department have to have a Data Science Team project Manager on staff?

822. Are your organizations Data Science Team

projects more successful over time?

823. Why is it to be done?

824. Does your organization have the means (staff, money, contract, etc.) to produce or to acquire the product, good, or service?

825. What specific interest groups do you have in place?

826. Are the attitudes of staff regarding Data Science Team project work improving?

827. How does this product, good, or service meet the needs of the Data Science Team project and your organization as a whole?

828. How can you make it practical?

829. Does the product, good, or service already exist within your organization?

830. Do you have an Enterprise Data Science Team project Management Office (EPMO)?

3.2 Change Request: Data Science Team

831. Have scm procedures for noting the change, recording it, and reporting it been followed?

832. Who is included in the change control team?

833. How are the measures for carrying out the change established?

834. Why were your requested changes rejected or not made?

835. How are changes requested (forms, method of communication)?

836. Will new change requests be acknowledged in a timely manner?

837. How do team members communicate with each other?

838. Why control change across the life cycle?

839. Are there requirements attributes that can discriminate between high and low reliability?

840. How does your organization control changes before and after software is released to a customer?

841. Who needs to approve change requests?

842. How do you get changes (code) out in a timely manner?

843. What are the requirements for urgent changes?

844. Has your address changed?

845. How shall the implementation of changes be recorded?

846. How are changes graded and who is responsible for the rating?

847. When to submit a change request?

848. Will all change requests and current status be logged?

849. Does the schedule include Data Science Team project management time and change request analysis time?

850. How many lines of code must be changed to implement the change?

3.3 Change Log: Data Science Team

851. Is the change request open, closed or pending?

852. Should a more thorough impact analysis be conducted?

853. Does the suggested change request represent a desired enhancement to the products functionality?

854. Is the submitted change a new change or a modification of a previously approved change?

855. Will the Data Science Team project fail if the change request is not executed?

856. Is the requested change request a result of changes in other Data Science Team project(s)?

857. Is this a mandatory replacement?

858. Is the change request within Data Science Team project scope?

859. How does this change affect the timeline of the schedule?

860. How does this relate to the standards developed for specific business processes?

861. Does the suggested change request seem to represent a necessary enhancement to the product?

862. When was the request approved?

863. When was the request submitted?

864. Where do changes come from?

865. Is the change backward compatible without limitations?

866. Do the described changes impact on the integrity or security of the system?

867. How does this change affect scope?

868. Who initiated the change request?

3.4 Decision Log: Data Science Team

869. Linked to original objective?

870. Who will be given a copy of this document and where will it be kept?

871. How do you know when you are achieving it?

872. How do you define success?

873. How does the use a Decision Support System influence the strategies/tactics or costs?

874. Decision-making process; how will the team make decisions?

875. What is the line where eDiscovery ends and document review begins?

876. Is your opponent open to a non-traditional workflow, or will it likely challenge anything you do?

877. Behaviors; what are guidelines that the team has identified that will assist them with getting the most out of team meetings?

878. Who is the decisionmaker?

879. What alternatives/risks were considered?

880. At what point in time does loss become unacceptable?

881. How does an increasing emphasis on cost containment influence the strategies and tactics used?

882. What was the rationale for the decision?

883. What are the cost implications?

884. How consolidated and comprehensive a story can you tell by capturing currently available incident data in a central location and through a log of key decisions during an incident?

885. How effective is maintaining the log at facilitating organizational learning?

886. What eDiscovery problem or issue did your organization set out to fix or make better?

887. What is the average size of your matters in an applicable measurement?

888. With whom was the decision shared or considered?

3.5 Quality Audit: Data Science Team

889. Are storage areas and reconditioning operations designed to prevent mix-ups and assure orderly handling of both the distressed and reconditioned devices?

890. How does your organization know that its staff embody the core knowledge, skills and characteristics for which it wishes to be recognized?

891. How does your organization know that its policy management system is appropriately effective and constructive?

892. How does your organization know that its security arrangements are appropriately effective and constructive?

893. Statements of intent remain exactly that until they are put into effect. The next step is to deploy the already stated intentions. In other words, do the plans happen in reality?

894. Is there a written corporate quality policy?

895. How does your organization know that the quality of its supervisors is appropriately effective and constructive?

896. How do you indicate the extent to which your personnel would be expected to contribute to the work effort?

897. Do the acceptance procedures and specifications include the criteria for acceptance/rejection, define the process to be used, and specify the measuring and test equipment that is to be used?

898. Is there a risk that information provided by management may not always be reliable?

899. What is your organizations greatest strength?

900. How does your organization know that its relationship with its (past) staff is appropriately effective and constructive?

901. Have the risks associated with the intentions been identified, analyzed and appropriate responses developed?

902. Is refuse and garbage adequately stored and disposed of with sufficient frequency to prevent contamination?

903. How does your organization know that its staffing profile is optimally aligned with the capability requirements implicit (or explicit) in its Strategic Plan?

904. Does everyone know what they are supposed to be doing, how and why?

905. Does the report read coherently?

906. Is your organizational structure a help or a hindrance to deployment?

907. How does your organization know that it is appropriately effective and constructive in preparing

its staff for organizational aspirations?

908. Are the intentions consistent with external obligations (such as applicable laws)?

3.6 Team Directory: Data Science Team

909. Who will report Data Science Team project status to all stakeholders?

910. Why is the work necessary?

911. Who are your stakeholders (customers, sponsors, end users, team members)?

912. When will you produce deliverables?

913. Does a Data Science Team project team directory list all resources assigned to the Data Science Team project?

914. Process decisions: is work progressing on schedule and per contract requirements?

915. Where should the information be distributed?

916. How does the team resolve conflicts and ensure tasks are completed?

917. How and in what format should information be presented?

918. Who will be the stakeholders on your next Data Science Team project?

919. How do unidentified risks impact the outcome of the Data Science Team project?

920. Process decisions: how well was task order work performed?

921. Process decisions: do job conditions warrant additional actions to collect job information and document on-site activity?

922. Decisions: is the most suitable form of contract being used?

923. Who are the Team Members?

924. Timing: when do the effects of communication take place?

925. Process decisions: do invoice amounts match accepted work in place?

926. Process decisions: are there any statutory or regulatory issues relevant to the timely execution of work?

927. Days from the time the issue is identified?

3.7 Team Operating Agreement: Data Science Team

928. Do you leverage technology engagement tools group chat, polls, screen sharing, etc.?

929. Did you recap the meeting purpose, time, and expectations?

930. Do you brief absent members after they view meeting notes or listen to a recording?

931. How will group handle unplanned absences?

932. Did you determine the technology methods that best match the messages to be communicated?

933. What is a Virtual Team?

934. Must your team members rely on the expertise of other members to complete tasks?

935. Are leadership responsibilities shared among team members (versus a single leader)?

936. Do you solicit member feedback about meetings and what would make them better?

937. How will your group handle planned absences?

938. How will you divide work equitably?

939. Do team members reside in more than two

countries?

940. Is compensation based on team and individual performance?

941. What are the safety issues/risks that need to be addressed and/or that the team needs to consider?

942. Do you vary your voice pace, tone and pitch to engage participants and gain involvement?

943. Has the appropriate access to relevant data and analysis capability been granted?

944. Conflict resolution: how will disputes and other conflicts be mediated or resolved?

945. Do you post meeting notes and the recording (if used) and notify participants?

946. Resource allocation: how will individual team members account for time and expenses, and how will this be allocated in the team budget?

947. Do you ensure that all participants know how to use the required technology?

3.8 Team Performance Assessment: Data Science Team

948. What structural changes have you made or are you preparing to make?

949. What do you think is the most constructive thing that could be done now to resolve considerations and disputes about method variance?

950. To what degree will the team adopt a concrete, clearly understood, and agreed-upon approach that will result in achievement of the teams goals?

951. How does Data Science Team project termination impact Data Science Team project team members?

952. To what degree do team members frequently explore the teams purpose and its implications?

953. To what degree can team members meet frequently enough to accomplish the teams ends?

954. To what degree will team members, individually and collectively, commit time to help themselves and others learn and develop skills?

955. Delaying market entry: how long is too long?

956. If you have criticized someones work for method variance in your role as reviewer, what was the circumstance?

957. To what degree does the teams work approach provide opportunity for members to engage in open interaction?

958. To what degree are the goals ambitious?

959. If you have received criticism from reviewers that your work suffered from method variance, what was the circumstance?

960. Does more radicalness mean more perceived benefits?

961. How hard did you try to make a good selection?

962. Do you give group members authority to make at least some important decisions?

963. How do you recognize and praise members for contributions?

964. To what degree does the teams purpose contain themes that are particularly meaningful and memorable?

965. To what degree do all members feel responsible for all agreed-upon measures?

966. To what degree will the team ensure that all members equitably share the work essential to the success of the team?

967. To what degree are the members clear on what they are individually responsible for and what they are jointly responsible for?

3.9 Team Member Performance Assessment: Data Science Team

968. Is it critical or vital to the job?

969. What is used as a basis for instructional decisions?

970. What is the large, desired outcome?

971. How should adaptive assessments be implemented?

972. Why were corresponding selected?

973. Does platform-specific assessment information contribute to training placement or tailoring of instruction (e.g. aptitude-treatment interaction)?

974. What are best practices for delivering and developing training evaluations to maximize the benefits of leveraging emerging technologies?

975. Who should attend?

976. Are the goals SMART ?

977. What steps have you taken to improve performance?

978. Verify business objectives. Are they appropriate, and well-articulated?

979. What are the standards or expectations for success?

980. How will they be formed?

981. What is the target group for instruction (e.g., individual and collective or small team instruction)?

982. What specific plans do you have for developing effective cross-platform assessments in a blended learning environment?

983. Does adaptive training work?

984. Who is responsible?

985. Do the goals support your organizations goals?

3.10 Issue Log: Data Science Team

986. Do you feel a register helps?

987. Which stakeholders can influence others?

988. Who is involved as you identify stakeholders?

989. Are the Data Science Team project issues uniquely identified, including to which product they refer?

990. What steps can you take for positive relationships?

991. Who reported the issue?

992. Why do you manage communications?

993. How do you reply to this question; you am new here and managing this major program. How do you suggest you build your network?

994. What is the impact on the risks?

995. Persistence; will users learn a work around or will they be bothered every time?

996. Who do you turn to if you have questions?

997. Who are the members of the governing body?

998. Who have you worked with in past, similar initiatives?

999. What is the status of the issue?

4.0 Monitoring and Controlling Process Group: Data Science Team

1000. How should needs be met?

1001. Is the program in place as intended?

1002. If a risk event occurs, what will you do?

1003. What is the expected monetary value of the Data Science Team project?

1004. How well did the team follow the chosen processes?

1005. Have operating capacities been created and/or reinforced in partners?

1006. Propriety: who needs to be involved in the evaluation to be ethical?

1007. What do they need to know about the Data Science Team project?

1008. Is there sufficient time allotted between the general system design and the detailed system design phases?

1009. Did you implement the program as designed?

1010. How well did the chosen processes fit the needs of the Data Science Team project?

1011. Do the partners have sufficient financial capacity to keep up the benefits produced by the programme?

1012. What will you do to minimize the impact should a risk event occur?

1013. Where is the Risk in the Data Science Team project?

1014. Did the Data Science Team project team have enough people to execute the Data Science Team project plan?

1015. How to ensure validity, quality and consistency?

1016. How well did you do?

1017. Is there undesirable impact on staff or resources?

4.1 Project Performance Report: Data Science Team

1018. To what degree are the structures of the formal organization consistent with the behaviors in the informal organization?

1019. To what degree do team members articulate the teams work approach?

1020. To what degree can all members engage in open and interactive considerations?

1021. To what degree does the teams work approach provide opportunity for members to engage in fact-based problem solving?

1022. To what degree are the skill areas critical to team performance present?

1023. To what degree will new and supplemental skills be introduced as the need is recognized?

1024. What is the degree to which rules govern information exchange between individuals within your organization?

1025. To what degree do the relationships of the informal organization motivate taskrelevant behavior and facilitate task completion?

1026. To what degree does the information network communicate information relevant to the task?

1027. To what degree does the teams approach to its work allow for modification and improvement over time?

1028. To what degree does the formal organization make use of individual resources and meet individual needs?

1029. To what degree do team members feel that the purpose of the team is important, if not exciting?

1030. What is the PRS?

1031. To what degree do team members agree with the goals, relative importance, and the ways in which achievement will be measured?

1032. To what degree are the tasks requirements reflected in the flow and storage of information?

1033. To what degree are fresh input and perspectives systematically caught and added (for example, through information and analysis, new members, and senior sponsors)?

1034. To what degree do members articulate the goals beyond the team membership?

1035. To what degree can the cognitive capacity of individuals accommodate the flow of information?

1036. What is in it for you?

4.2 Variance Analysis: Data Science Team

1037. Is the entire contract planned in time-phased control accounts to the extent practicable?

1038. Are authorized changes being incorporated in a timely manner?

1039. How have the setting and use of standards changed over time?

1040. Are management actions taken to reduce indirect costs when there are significant adverse variances?

1041. Can the contractor substantiate work package and planning package budgets?

1042. Are your organizations and items of cost assigned to each pool identified?

1043. Is there a logical explanation for any variance?

1044. Do the rates and prices remain constant throughout the year?

1045. Is the market likely to continue to grow at this rate next year?

1046. Are the wbs and organizational levels for application of the Data Science Team projected overhead costs identified?

1047. Budget versus actual. how does the monthly budget compare to actual experience?

1048. Can the relationship with problem customers be restructured so that there is a win-win situation?

1049. What is the incurrence of actual indirect costs in excess of budgets, by element of expense?

1050. Are the bases and rates for allocating costs from each indirect pool consistently applied?

1051. What is the actual cost of work performed?

1052. Did a new competitor enter the market?

4.3 Earned Value Status: Data Science Team

1053. How much is it going to cost by the finish?

1054. If earned value management (EVM) is so good in determining the true status of a Data Science Team project and Data Science Team project its completion, why is it that hardly any one uses it in information systems related Data Science Team projects?

1055. Are you hitting your Data Science Team projects targets?

1056. Where is evidence-based earned value in your organization reported?

1057. Validation is a process of ensuring that the developed system will actually achieve the stakeholders desired outcomes; Are you building the right product? What do you validate?

1058. Earned value can be used in almost any Data Science Team project situation and in almost any Data Science Team project environment. it may be used on large Data Science Team projects, medium sized Data Science Team projects, tiny Data Science Team projects (in cut-down form), complex and simple Data Science Team projects and in any market sector. some people, of course, know all about earned value, they have used it for years - but perhaps not as effectively as they could have?

1059. Where are your problem areas?

1060. How does this compare with other Data Science Team projects?

1061. When is it going to finish?

1062. What is the unit of forecast value?

1063. Verification is a process of ensuring that the developed system satisfies the stakeholders agreements and specifications; Are you building the product right? What do you verify?

4.4 Risk Audit: Data Science Team

1064. Does your organization have or has considered the need for insurance covers: public liability, professional indemnity and directors and officers liability?

1065. Have permissions or required permits to use facilities managed by other parties been obtained?

1066. What does internal control mean in the context of the audit process?

1067. Strategic business risk audit methodologies; are corresponding an attempt to sell other services, and is management becoming the client of the audit rather than the shareholder?

1068. Is the process supported by tools?

1069. Is the number of people on the Data Science Team project team adequate to do the job?

1070. Do you have written and signed agreements/contracts in place for each paid staff member?

1071. Are audit program plans risk-adjusted?

1072. How effective are your risk controls?

1073. Do you have a clear plan for the future that describes what you want to do and how you are going to do it?

1074. Does the implementation method matter?

1075. What risk does not having unique identification present?

1076. How do you govern assets?

1077. Does your auditor understand your business?

1078. Management -what contingency plans do you have if the risk becomes a reality?

1079. Does the Data Science Team project team have experience with the technology to be implemented?

1080. Estimated size of product in number of programs, files, transactions?

1081. Do you have an emergency plan?

1082. Do you manage the process through use of metrics?

4.5 Contractor Status Report: Data Science Team

1083. What is the average response time for answering a support call?

1084. What are the minimum and optimal bandwidth requirements for the proposed solution?

1085. What was the final actual cost?

1086. What was the actual budget or estimated cost for your organizations services?

1087. How does the proposed individual meet each requirement?

1088. How long have you been using the services?

1089. What process manages the contracts?

1090. If applicable; describe your standard schedule for new software version releases. Are new software version releases included in the standard maintenance plan?

1091. How is risk transferred?

1092. Who can list a Data Science Team project as organization experience, your organization or a previous employee of your organization?

1093. Describe how often regular updates are made

to the proposed solution. Are corresponding regular updates included in the standard maintenance plan?

1094. What was the overall budget or estimated cost?

1095. What was the budget or estimated cost for your organizations services?

1096. Are there contractual transfer concerns?

4.6 Formal Acceptance: Data Science Team

1097. What lessons were learned about your Data Science Team project management methodology?

1098. Is formal acceptance of the Data Science Team project product documented and distributed?

1099. What is the Acceptance Management Process?

1100. Was the Data Science Team project goal achieved?

1101. Was business value realized?

1102. Have all comments been addressed?

1103. How does your team plan to obtain formal acceptance on your Data Science Team project?

1104. General estimate of the costs and times to complete the Data Science Team project?

1105. Did the Data Science Team project achieve its MOV?

1106. What are the requirements against which to test, Who will execute?

1107. Do you perform formal acceptance or burn-in tests?

1108. Was the sponsor/customer satisfied?

1109. Do you buy-in installation services?

1110. Was the Data Science Team project work done on time, within budget, and according to specification?

1111. How well did the team follow the methodology?

1112. Was the Data Science Team project managed well?

1113. What was done right?

1114. What features, practices, and processes proved to be strengths or weaknesses?

1115. Do you buy pre-configured systems or build your own configuration?

1116. Was the client satisfied with the Data Science Team project results?

5.0 Closing Process Group: Data Science Team

1117. What areas were overlooked on this Data Science Team project?

1118. What areas does the group agree are the biggest success on the Data Science Team project?

1119. What was learned?

1120. Is the Data Science Team project funded?

1121. Is this an updated Data Science Team project Proposal Document?

1122. What could be done to improve the process?

1123. What can you do better next time, and what specific actions can you take to improve?

1124. Just how important is your work to the overall success of the Data Science Team project?

1125. Were cost budgets met?

1126. Were the outcomes different from the already stated planned?

1127. How well did the chosen processes fit the needs of the Data Science Team project?

1128. Did the delivered product meet the specified

requirements and goals of the Data Science Team project?

1129. Were risks identified and mitigated?

1130. How will you know you did it?

1131. What is the risk of failure to your organization?

1132. Specific - is the objective clear in terms of what, how, when, and where the situation will be changed?

1133. What is the Data Science Team project Management Process?

5.1 Procurement Audit: Data Science Team

1134. Are eu procurement regulations applicable?

1135. Are the number of checking accounts where cash segregation is not required kept to a reasonable number?

1136. Was the submission of variant tenders accepted and duly ruled?

1137. Is the minutes book kept current?

1138. Were additional works strictly necessary for the completion of performance under the contract?

1139. Were there no material changes in the contract shortly after award?

1140. When you set social or environmental conditions for the performance of the contract, were corresponding compatible with the law and was adequate information given to the candidates?

1141. Are travel expenditures monitored to determine that they are in line with other employees and reasonable for the area of travel?

1142. Are checks used in numeric sequence?

1143. Is there a procedure to summarize bids and select a vendor?

1144. Are open purchase orders with a fixed monetary limitation used for local purchases of small dollar value?

1145. How do you assess whether the technical and financial evaluation was done properly and in fair manner?

1146. Are the users needs clearly and invariably defined and has the expected outcome or mission been clearly identified and communicated in measurable terms?

1147. Who are the key suppliers?

1148. If a purchase order calls for a cost-plus agreement, is the method of determining how final charges will be determined specified?

1149. When performance conditions were detailed in the tender documentation, did the contracting authority verify if the tenders received met the already stated requirements?

1150. Is there no evidence of false certifications?

1151. Is there no evidence of favouritism towards a particular contractor during the evaluation and negotiation processes?

1152. Where your organization engaged an expert, was the contract awarded in compliance with procurement regulations?

1153. Are regulations on taxes, fees, duties, excises,

tariffs etc. not impeding (international) competition?

5.2 Contract Close-Out: Data Science Team

1154. How/when used ?

1155. Was the contract type appropriate?

1156. Was the contract complete without requiring numerous changes and revisions?

1157. How does it work?

1158. Have all contract records been included in the Data Science Team project archives?

1159. Why Outsource?

1160. Change in circumstances?

1161. Have all contracts been closed?

1162. What is capture management?

1163. Are the signers the authorized officials?

1164. Have all contracts been completed?

1165. Change in knowledge?

1166. How is the contracting office notified of the automatic contract close-out?

1167. Was the contract sufficiently clear so as not to

result in numerous disputes and misunderstandings?

1168. Parties: who is involved?

1169. Has each contract been audited to verify acceptance and delivery?

1170. Change in attitude or behavior?

1171. Have all acceptance criteria been met prior to final payment to contractors?

1172. Parties: Authorized?

1173. What happens to the recipient of services?

5.3 Project or Phase Close-Out: Data Science Team

1174. Who are the Data Science Team project stakeholders and what are roles and involvement?

1175. Planned completion date?

1176. In preparing the Lessons Learned report, should it reflect a consensus viewpoint, or should the report reflect the different individual viewpoints?

1177. Complete yes or no?

1178. If you were the Data Science Team project sponsor, how would you determine which Data Science Team project team(s) and/or individuals deserve recognition?

1179. What could have been improved?

1180. What process was planned for managing issues/risks?

1181. What were the goals and objectives of the communications strategy for the Data Science Team project?

1182. What benefits or impacts does the stakeholder group expect to obtain as a result of the Data Science Team project?

1183. What is this stakeholder expecting?

1184. How much influence did the stakeholder have over others?

1185. What is the information level of detail required for each stakeholder?

1186. Does the lesson describe a function that would be done differently the next time?

1187. Was the user/client satisfied with the end product?

1188. Did the delivered product meet the specified requirements and goals of the Data Science Team project?

1189. Were messages directly related to the release strategy or phases of the Data Science Team project?

5.4 Lessons Learned: Data Science Team

1190. How was the Data Science Team project controlled?

1191. Was there enough support – guidance, clerical support, training?

1192. What are the expectations of the individuals?

1193. Did the Data Science Team project management methodology work?

1194. What is the supplier dependency?

1195. Where could you improve?

1196. For the next Data Science Team project, how could you improve on the way Data Science Team project was conducted?

1197. How accurately and timely was the Risk Management Log updated or reviewed?

1198. Are new goals needed?

1199. Why do you need to measure?

1200. What skills are required for the task?

1201. How effective were your design reviews?

1202. Which estimation issues did you personally have and what was the impact?

1203. What are the funding priorities for intelligence?

1204. How effective was the documentation that you received with the Data Science Team project product/ service?

1205. Was the necessary hardware, software, accommodation etc available?

1206. How effective was the architecture/system design process?

1207. What are the needs of the individuals?

1208. Do you have any real problems?

1209. Was Data Science Team project performance validated or challenged?

Index

assign 19
assigned   129, 149, 151, 172-173, 190, 225, 239
Assignment   4, 158, 186
assist   8, 69, 93, 177, 220
assistant   7
associated   152-153, 207, 223
Assumption   3, 147
assurance   16, 172, 188, 190, 212
assure 222
attached   169
attainable   40, 167, 188
attempt   243
attempted   30
attempting   99
attend 17, 231
attendance   35
attended   35
attention   11, 104, 194
attitude   255
attitudes   215
attributes   3, 111, 141-142, 157, 216
audience   211
audiences   211
audited   255
auditing   22, 97, 115, 186
auditor 244
audits 180
author 1
authority   71, 139, 151, 187, 193, 230, 252
authorized   135, 151-152, 239, 254-255
automatic   254
available   20, 22, 28, 55, 66, 68, 85, 93, 122, 153, 155, 157,
170, 182, 194, 196, 198, 200, 210, 213, 221, 259
Average   11, 26, 41, 56, 73, 88, 100, 124, 190, 221, 245
avoided   166
awarded   252
awareness   132
background   9
backward   219
balanced   77
bandwidth   245
barriers 122
baseline   4, 110, 138, 146, 178, 190

considered   17, 20, 50, 220-221, 243
considers   69
consist 151
consistent   36, 43, 63, 92, 224, 237
constant   239
constantly   193
Constraint   3, 147
consultant   7, 174
consulted   109
consulting   52
consumers   116
contact   7, 191, 205
contacts   104
contain   24, 70, 91, 230
contained   1, 151
contains   8
content   36
contents   1-2, 8
context   30, 33, 36, 39, 213, 243
continual   91, 94
continue   239
continuity   45
continuous   58, 78
contract   6, 151-153, 167, 186, 215, 225-226, 239, 251-252, 254-255
contractor   6, 152, 174, 239, 245, 252
contracts   41, 70, 152, 159, 166, 208, 243, 245, 254
contribute   222, 231
control 2, 36, 49, 63, 89-93, 97-98, 100, 127, 132, 146, 151, 167, 176, 213, 216, 239, 243
controlled   66, 258
controls   24, 68, 77, 80, 84, 91, 94, 96-97, 99-100, 138, 161, 196, 202, 243
convention   113
convey   1
convince   187, 190
cooperate   177
Copyright   1
corporate   222
correct42, 89, 171
corrective   53, 99, 172
correspond   8-9
cosmetic   147

272

edition 8
editorial   1
education   19, 89
effect 197, 201, 222
effective   17, 19, 112, 115, 117, 142, 168, 203, 221-223, 232, 243, 258-259
effects 131, 134, 226
efficiency   59, 97
efficient   46, 75, 133, 214
effort   39, 46-47, 51, 187, 191, 222
efforts 30, 76, 129, 148
Electrical   147
electronic   1
element   152, 240
elements   9, 32, 66, 99, 122, 145, 151-153, 173, 184, 186-187, 212
elicit   184
eliminated   148
embarking   34
embody   222
embrace   210
emergency   244
emergent   52
emerging   62, 98, 231
emphasis   221
employee   106, 245
employees   17, 21, 24, 67, 119, 121, 123, 190, 251
employers   130
empower   7
enable 59
enablers   118
encourage   75, 91
engage   121, 192, 228, 230, 237
engaged   252
engagement 55, 130, 192, 227
Engineers   147
enhance   96
enhanced   103
enhancing   93
enough   7, 61, 104, 115, 123, 140-141, 144, 173, 212, 229, 236, 258
ensure 29, 37, 69, 72, 112, 120-121, 138, 173, 180, 185, 189, 225, 228, 230, 236

process 1-7, 9, 28-30, 33, 35, 40, 55, 58-72, 89-91, 93-95, 98-99, 126, 133-134, 136, 139-140, 142-143, 145-148, 163, 166-167, 184-185, 190, 195, 197, 200-201, 208, 211-212, 220, 223, 225-226, 235, 241-245, 247, 249-250, 256, 259

processes 45, 49, 57-59, 61, 63-65, 68-69, 71-72, 92, 94, 98-99, 133, 148, 153, 205, 209-210, 212-213, 218, 235, 248-249, 252

produce 64, 71, 163, 213, 215, 225

produced 64, 84, 146, 236

produces 157

producing 143

product 1, 50, 60, 70, 102, 104, 140, 145, 159, 178-179, 194-195, 212, 215, 218, 233, 241-242, 244, 247, 249, 257, 259

production 33, 84, 122

products 1, 16, 65, 128, 133-134, 143, 174, 214, 218

profile 223

profit 182

profits 178

program 19, 72, 99, 128, 133-134, 233, 235, 243

programme 236

programs 214, 244

progress 27, 45, 83, 92, 121, 129, 131, 133-134, 153, 176, 184-185, 213

project 2-8, 19-20, 22, 24, 41, 55, 64-65, 70, 86, 89-91, 102, 105, 107, 111, 113, 120-122, 125-131, 133-141, 143, 145-146, 148-150, 153, 155-158, 160-162, 164-174, 176-181, 183, 186, 188, 190-191, 194, 196-200, 204-206, 208-209, 212-215, 217-218, 225, 229, 233, 235-237, 241, 243-245, 247-250, 254, 256-259

projected 152, 179, 186-187, 239

projects 2, 49, 103, 119, 125-126, 134, 143, 145, 149, 166, 187, 191, 198, 201, 213-215, 241-242

promising 102

promote 60

proper 96, 154

properly 32, 40, 127, 252

proponents 193

Proposal 160, 249

proposals 167, 206

proposed 19, 48, 52, 135, 141, 196, 206-207, 209-210, 245-246

Propriety 235

protect 112

protected 71

protection 107

readiness   33, 173
readings   96, 133
realistic   21, 69, 111
reality 222, 244
realize 43
realized   114, 247
really   7, 24, 33
reason 110, 114, 197
reasonable   85, 108, 135, 153, 204, 251
reasons   34
reassess   208
rebuild 102
receive   8-9, 38, 52, 131
received   27, 123, 230, 252, 259
recently   108
recipient   25, 255
recognised   81
recognize   2, 15-16, 18-19, 23-24, 54, 79, 82, 87, 166, 230
recognized   16-17, 20, 23-25, 61, 222, 237
recognizes   22
recommend   110, 118, 145
record 181
recorded   138, 217
recording   1, 216, 227-228
records   68, 122, 151-152, 186, 254
recovery   45, 148
recurrence   203
redefine   21, 34
re-design   64
reduce 45, 50, 148, 197, 239
reduced   202
reducing   98, 107
referenced   182
references   260
reflect 66, 95, 99, 256
reflected   238
reform 50, 112, 124
reforms 19, 43, 52
refuse   223
regarding   109, 113, 147, 215
Register   2, 4, 130, 139, 196-197, 233
regret   84
regular 27, 35, 61, 245-246

services   1, 31, 46, 52, 111-112, 132, 174, 196, 243, 245-246, 248, 255
session 156
setbacks   69
setting 103, 111, 239
several 69
severely   64
shared 92, 95, 141, 177, 221, 227
sharing 75, 96, 210, 227
shifts   26, 200
shortly 251
should 7, 16-17, 20, 26, 35, 37, 40, 49, 52-53, 59-61, 65, 67, 69, 75, 83, 88-89, 97, 105, 109, 113, 118, 120, 126, 130, 134, 137, 139, 156-157, 159, 165, 168, 170-171, 174, 189, 194, 196-197, 206-207, 218, 225, 231, 235-236, 256
-should 178
signature   120
signatures   163
signed 243
signers 254
signing 181
similar   30, 41, 60, 71, 86, 157, 175, 233
simple 113, 241
Simply 8
single   123, 227
single-use   7
situation   18, 42, 196, 240-241, 250
situations   94
skeptical   116
skills   16, 21, 61, 107, 111, 121, 153, 190, 196, 209, 222, 229, 237, 258
slippage   201
smallest   20, 84
social 116, 202, 251
societal   114
society 200
software   16, 140, 166-167, 194, 212, 216, 245, 259
solicit   34, 167, 227
solution   55, 66, 69, 74, 77, 79-80, 82, 84, 86-87, 89, 202, 245-246
solutions   55, 75-77, 86, 196
solved 26
solving 237